INSIDER'S ENCYCLOPEDIA
ANIMALS

Silver Dolphin Books
An imprint of Printers Row Publishing Group
A division of Readerlink Distribution Services, LLC
10350 Barnes Canyon Road, Suite 100, San Diego, CA 92121
www.silverdolphinbooks.com

Copyright 2019 © Discovery Communications, LLC. Discovery™ and the Discovery™ logo
are trademarks of Discovery Communications, LLC, used under license.

All rights reserved. No part of this publication may be reproduced, distributed, or
transmitted in any form or by any means, including photocopying, recording, or other
electronic or mechanical methods, without the prior written permission of the publisher,
except in the case of brief quotations embodied in critical reviews and certain other
noncommercial uses permitted by copyright law.

Printers Row Publishing Group is a division of Readerlink Distribution Services, LLC.
Silver Dolphin Books is a registered trademark of Readerlink Distribution Services, LLC.

All notations of errors or omissions should be addressed to Silver Dolphin Books,
Editorial Department, at the above address.

ISBN: 978-1-68412-898-3

Manufactured, printed, and assembled in Heshan, China.
LP/10/19
23 22 21 20 19   1 2 3 4 5

Written by Dan Elish
Consultants: Bob Hirshon & Hazel Davies

Interiors designed, produced, and packaged by Big Yellow Taxi, Inc.

Discovery™

INSIDER'S ENCYCLOPEDIA
ANIMALS

Silver Dolphin

CONTENTS

ON LAND

BY AIR

AT SEA

AT HOME

Lions

KING OF THE BEASTS

There are many reasons that lions are one of the most feared predators on the planet. Predators are animals that hunt and eat other animals, and lions are built for hunting. Lion vision is about the same as humans' during the day. At night, their eyes are about six times more light-sensitive than ours. Their sharp hearing is boosted by ears that can turn in the direction of any noise. Their teeth can rip flesh and crush bones, and they can open their jaws nearly 1 foot (30 centimeters) wide, giving them one of the biggest bites in the animal kingdom. Lions truly are an apex predator, which means they are at the top of the food chain!

LIONS IN **TROUBLE**

Lions once roamed the Earth, roaring their way through Europe, Africa, the Middle East, North America, and northern India. Today most of the world's lions live in Africa. The last remaining Asiatic lions, about 500, are in Sasan-Gir National Park in India. This is a wildlife sanctuary where the animals are protected from harm. Scientists fear that some types of lions may one day become extinct. As a result, certain lions are on the endangered species list. This means that it is now illegal to hunt them or to destroy their habitats.

Asiatic Lions

DID YOU KNOW?

- A lion can run short distances at 50 mph (80 kph).
- A lion can leap as far as 36 ft (11 m).
- A lion needs lots of rest. Some sleep up to 20 hours a day.
- A lion's roar can be heard from as far as 5 miles (8 km) away.
- A male lion shows his power in his mane. The darker the mane, the more dominant the lion.

- Tigers have stripes on both their fur and skin. No two tigers have the same stripes.
- A tiger can see six times better at night than humans can.
- Unlike most cats, tigers are excellent swimmers. Their partially webbed paws help them navigate wide rivers.

STRIPED AND DEADLY!
Tigers

Another big cat and apex predator, tigers are solitary creatures, preferring to stick to themselves. Their dark stripes camouflage the big cats in grass and trees as they stalk their prey. The biggest of the big cats, the Siberian tiger can be as long as a car, and males can weigh up to 700 pounds (318 kilograms)!

Many cultures consider the tiger a symbol of power and courage because of its incredible size, strength, and beauty.

MEALTIME

When it comes to food, tigers don't mess around. These meat-eating cats hunt large prey such as deer, pigs, rhinos, and baby elephants. After killing their prey, the tiger chows down, sometimes eating 80 pounds (36 kilograms) or more of meat in one very long sitting. Now that's a meal!

GOES WITH THE TERRITORY

Tigers mark their territory by scratching their claws into trees and spraying the tree with their urine, just like domestic cats do. They live in a wide range of habitats, from rain forests to savannas to mangrove swamps. Their territory has been shrinking, though, and up to 93 percent of tigers' natural habitat has been destroyed by human activity. This loss of habitat, combined with illegal hunting, means there are now fewer than 4,000 tigers left in the wild. Three tiger subspecies are completely extinct, one is thought to be extinct in the wild, and the remaining five are endangered.

SNOW WHITE

White tigers are actually Bengal tigers born to two parents carrying a specific gene. This gene gives them white fur and blue eyes. There are only about 200 white tigers left in the world and it has been nearly 60 years since one has been spotted in the wild.

The cheetah gets its name from the Hindi word *chita*, meaning "spotted" or "sprinkled."

The fastest human sprinters can run about 23 miles (37 kilometers) per hour. A racing greyhound can fly past them at 42 miles (68 kilometers) per hour, and a racehorse can gallop by at 50 miles (80 kilometers) per hour. But a cheetah leaves them all in the dust! With the ability to accelerate from 0 to 45 miles (0 to 72 kilometers) per hour in only two seconds and to reach speeds of 70 miles (113 kilometers) per hour, the cheetah holds the world record for fastest land animal.

Cheetahs
FULL SPEED AHEAD

DID YOU **KNOW?**

Most cats' claws stay fully inside the paws unless the cat needs to use them. A cheetah's claws are different, though. Cheetahs need to take off on the spot, so their claws never fully retract. They help the cheetah grip the ground firmly and avoid slipping—kind of like nature's own football cleats!

Here's why the cheetah is the fastest land animal on the planet.

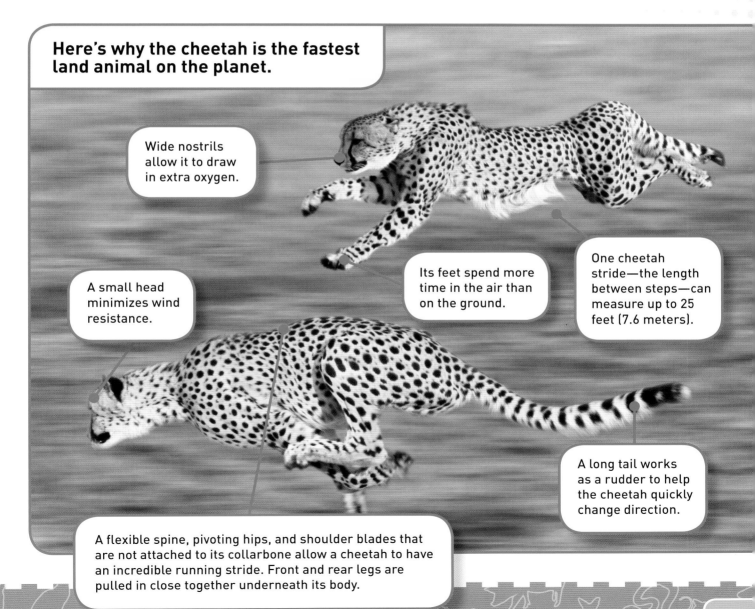

Wide nostrils allow it to draw in extra oxygen.

A small head minimizes wind resistance.

Its feet spend more time in the air than on the ground.

One cheetah stride—the length between steps—can measure up to 25 feet (7.6 meters).

A long tail works as a rudder to help the cheetah quickly change direction.

A flexible spine, pivoting hips, and shoulder blades that are not attached to its collarbone allow a cheetah to have an incredible running stride. Front and rear legs are pulled in close together underneath its body.

DID YOU KNOW?

There are nine subspecies of leopards, including the African, Persian, Amur, Indian, Javan, and North-Chinese leopard. Unfortunately, the Amur leopard, which lives in parts of Russia, China, and the Korean Peninsula, is critically endangered due to habitat loss and being hunted by humans. Today, there may be fewer than 70 wild Amur leopards left in the world!

Amur Leopard

Leopards and Jaguars

A TALE OF TWO KITTIES

Do you like climbing trees? If you're hiking in the African savanna or a South American rain forest, you'll have to be careful before climbing one. You might find a leopard or jaguar waiting for you! Unlike lions, tigers, and cheetahs, leopards are comfortable up high in leafy branches where they can keep an eye out for dinner. When hunting, these big cats often spring right out of a tree directly onto their prey's back. Jaguars have been spotted attacking prey from the trees, too. Of course, leopards and jaguars aren't always tree-bound. They also hit the ground to stalk their prey.

JUNGLE CAT

The jaguar is the largest cat in the Americas and the third largest in the world (after the tiger and lion). They are one of the few cats besides tigers who don't avoid water. That's because they're great swimmers! Jaguars currently roam South and Central America, with the biggest jaguar population found in the Amazon rain forest. They had been found in the United States, until hunters drove them away in the 1940s. But they may be coming back. Recently, there have been jaguar sightings in Arizona.

Jaguar

Leopard

Jaguar

LEOPARD OR JAGUAR?

LEOPARD	JAGUAR
• Found in Asia, the Middle East, and Africa	• Found in North, Central, and South America
• Fur has smaller rosettes with no central spot	• Fur has large rosettes with spots in the middle
• Bite a little more powerful than a dog	• One of the most powerful bites of all mammals
• Long, slight body with long tail	• Short, stocky body with shorter tail
• Do not like water	• Are strong swimmers

FUN FACTS!

- Each one of a tarsier's eyes is as big as its brain.
- Apes can easily catch colds from humans.

Primates
WHAT ARE THEY?

Primates have larger brains than most mammals, relative to their size. They have excellent vision, with eyes that sit close together and look straight forward. Primates have flat fingernails instead of claws, and most primates have opposable thumbs that allow them to grab and hold objects. Humans are primates, and so are our closest living relatives, apes and monkeys. Sadly, we're the only primates that can't grip things with our feet, too.

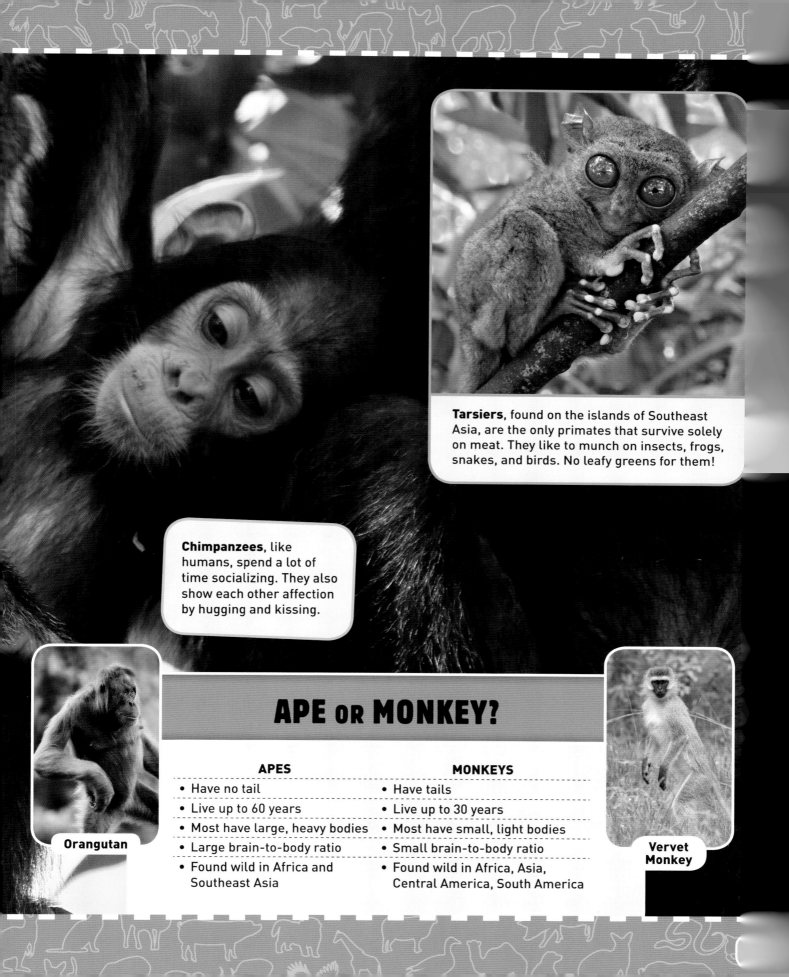

Tarsiers, found on the islands of Southeast Asia, are the only primates that survive solely on meat. They like to munch on insects, frogs, snakes, and birds. No leafy greens for them!

Chimpanzees, like humans, spend a lot of time socializing. They also show each other affection by hugging and kissing.

APE or MONKEY?

APES	MONKEYS
• Have no tail	• Have tails
• Live up to 60 years	• Live up to 30 years
• Most have large, heavy bodies	• Most have small, light bodies
• Large brain-to-body ratio	• Small brain-to-body ratio
• Found wild in Africa and Southeast Asia	• Found wild in Africa, Asia, Central America, South America

Orangutan

Vervet Monkey

LEADER OF THE BAND

Bands of gorillas are led by a dominant male called a silverback. You can spot this gorilla by the gray whoosh of hair on his back. Silverbacks have a lot of responsibility. They have to make decisions, find new sites for food, resolve conflicts, and defend their territory.

Silverback

Gorillas

GENTLE GIANTS

Rain Forest

Africa

They are big. They are strong. They can grow over 6 feet (2 meters) tall and can weigh nearly 500 pounds (227 kilograms). They are gorillas, the largest primates on the planet. There are two species of these magnificent and surprisingly gentle creatures, the eastern and the western gorilla, both found in Africa. There, you're most likely to spot a Western Lowland Gorilla. There are between 100,000 and 200,000 of them living in African rain forests. You'll have a much harder time finding the Western Cross River Gorilla that lives in the forests of Nigeria and Cameroon. There are only about 300 of them left. Gorillas live in groups of about 20 to 30, called troops or bands. The males, about one to four in each troop, protect the females and young gorillas.

DID YOU KNOW?

Apes don't have the ability to speak like humans, but they can communicate. A gorilla named Koko learned sign language. She can use over a thousand signs, and has even combined signs to make up new words. When Koko saw a zebra, she signed "white" and "tiger" to describe it!

ALMOST HUMAN?

Gorillas are closely related to humans. In fact, 98 percent of gorilla DNA is identical to that of *Homo sapiens* (a fancy word for you and me). Like humans, female gorillas are pregnant for nine months and usually produce one baby at a time. Gorillas like to keep a schedule. They forage for food in the morning and evening, nap and wash during the day, then sleep in beds made out of leaves and branches at night.

STRICTLY
VEGETARIAN

No question about it: A beast as strong and fierce-looking as a gorilla has to eat meat, right? Guess again. Gorillas are primarily herbivores. They like snacking on bamboo, leafy plants, and fruit. Some will snack on an occasional insect, though. It takes a lot to keep one of these big apes going. An adult gorilla can eat upward of 40 pounds (18 kilograms) of food a day!

Monkeys

WHAT DO THEY SEE?
WHAT DO THEY DO?

Spider monkeys live in the tropical rain forests of South America. During the day they hang out in small groups of two to eight monkeys, but their social groups have up to 25 individuals in them.

Close your eyes and picture a monkey. Is it as small as a squirrel? As big as you? It could be either, or anywhere in between! There are 260 different species of monkeys in the world today. The smallest, South America's pygmy marmoset, weighs in at 3.5 ounces (100 grams). On the other end of the scale is Africa's mandrill, which weighs around 77 pounds (35 kilograms). While all monkeys can use their hands and feet to grab and hold, they have many different characteristics, depending on their habitats. Monkeys have been around for more than 50 million years, but scientists still aren't exactly sure how so many different species of monkeys evolved.

Old World monkeys, such as mandrills and baboons, are found in Africa and Asia. They have cheek pouches where they can stuff food to eat later on. New World monkeys, such as pygmy marmosets and spider monkeys, have prehensile tails that can hold onto things. This helps them travel through trees and keeps their hands free to grab food to eat!

CHIT-CHIT-CHITTY-CHAT

You may not understand what monkeys are chatting about, but they are communicating. Monkeys use a variety of calls, clicks, cackles, squeaks, and screeches to have conversations, arguments, and deliver warnings. Diana monkeys are some of the best communicators in the monkey world. They can combine calls to make messages that are like human sentences. They can even understand the calls of other monkey species!

FUNNY LOOKING? DON'T TELL THEM THAT!

Mandrill

Male mandrills have some of the most colorful faces in the mammal world—and their colors get even brighter when they're excited.

Proboscis Monkey

You might look at this proboscis monkey and think it has an amazing sense of smell. But you'd be wrong! This male monkey has a long nose because it looks attractive to the lady monkeys.

Emperor Tamarin

Emperor tamarins aren't rulers of all monkeys, but their white mustaches may have reminded explorers of the German emperor Wilhelm II.

IT'S NOT AN EARTHQUAKE . . .
HERE COME THE
Elephants

Weighing as much as seven tons (6.3 metric tons), an elephant, the largest land mammal, can balance a scale with almost 80 humans on the other side. Even a newborn baby elephant weighs over 200 pounds (91 kilograms), which is larger than the average adult human. Elephants live in groups called herds. Each herd is led by the matriarch, or oldest female. While female elephants stay with the herd their whole lives, male elephants are expected to head out on their own at a young age. Plant eaters, or herbivores, elephants eat grass, fruit, roots, and bark. Both African and Asian elephants need wide areas of land to roam in order to find the huge amounts of food they need to survive.

SUNBURN?

Elephant skin is 1 inch (2.5 cm) thick, but they are still sensitive to sunlight. Humans use sunscreen. Elephants coat their skin with mud or dust.

NAME THAT TUSK

Are you right-handed? Left-handed? Just like humans favor one or the other hand, elephants favor one or the other of their tusks, making them right-tusked or left-tusked. Over time, the dominant tusk gets more worn down than the less-used one.

PACKING A TRUNK

An elephant packs a lot of tasks into its impressively large trunk:

• It uses its trunk to breathe, smell, blow water into its mouth, and to communicate. Elephants can bark, rumble, grunt, cry, and trumpet loudly

• An elephant's trunk has more than 40,000 muscles and can hold more tha 2 gal (7.6 L) of water! It's strong enough to pick up a tree trunk, and delic enough to crack open a peanut shell.

• When elephants meet, they often extend their trunks in greeting.

Giraffes
A VIEW FROM THE TOP

Reaching almost 20 feet (6 meters) in height, the giraffe is the tallest animal in the African grasslands— and in the world! Its neck alone is 6 feet (2 meters) long and is bigger than the average-size man. The giraffe's powerful heart is enormous and weighs almost 25 pounds (11 kilograms). With a tongue that can stretch up to 1.5 feet (0.5 meters), this graceful animal can grab and eat leaves from the tippy-tops of trees.

FUN FACT!

Sometimes male giraffes fight each other by slamming necks, an activity called necking. They hit each other so hard the smacks can be heard up to 0.5 miles (1 kilometer) away!

POWER NAPPERS, FAST RUNNERS

In order to keep an eye out for predators in the wild, giraffes nap for only about five minutes at a time, up to four hours a day total, and almost always standing up. From their view above the savanna, giraffes can usually spot a predator in time to run away—and they are quick. A giraffe can sprint up to 35 miles (56 kilometers) per hour.

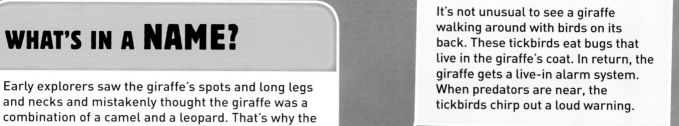

WHAT'S IN A NAME?

Early explorers saw the giraffe's spots and long legs and necks and mistakenly thought the giraffe was a combination of a camel and a leopard. That's why the ancient Romans called giraffes "camel-leopards," and why one giraffe species is called *camelopardalis*.

BIRD WATCHING?

It's not unusual to see a giraffe walking around with birds on its back. These tickbirds eat bugs that live in the giraffe's coat. In return, the giraffe gets a live-in alarm system. When predators are near, the tickbirds chirp out a loud warning.

Zebras
IT'S ALL IN BLACK AND WHITE

Zebras belong to the *Equus* genus—just like horses and donkeys do.

When lions see herds of zebra roaming the African savanna, they see a tasty meal. But they'd better be ready to run for it! Three species of zebras roam the grasslands— Grevy's, mountain, and plains. They keep a constant eye out for predators, and when they see one, they can really tear up the turf. A zebra can zigzag at a gallop of 40 miles (64 kilometers) per hour. That's faster than an average lion, and even baby zebras can keep up with the herd a few hours after birth. Plains and mountain zebras spend most of their time in small groups called harems. The small groups join together in large herds for protection. Grevy's zebras only come together in groups for brief periods of time. Zebras communicate with each other with sounds and expressions. If one spots a lion, it will make a loud noise to warn the rest of the harem.

SHOW YOUR STRIPES!

- Zebras living in warmer climates tend to have more stripes.
- A zebra's skin is solid black underneath its striped coat.
- Just as every human has a unique set of fingerprints, every zebra has a set of stripes to call its very own. A foal can even recognize its mother by the pattern of her stripes.
- Zebras are born with brown and white stripes. After a few months the brown stripes turn black.

MISTAKEN IDENTITY

In Ancient Rome, zebras were used to pull chariots at circuses. The Romans called them *hippotigris* or "horse-tigers."

RECORD BREAKERS

- The royal antelope is about the size of a rabbit. It weighs only 5.5 lbs (2.5 kg).

- The giant spiral-horned eland can weigh nearly 1 ton (0.9 MT)!

- The pronghorn antelope can reach speeds of 55 mph (89 kph).

- Impalas can spring nearly 10 ft (3 m) into the air, likely higher than any other antelope!

Antelope

HANDSOME HORNS ON DISPLAY

Antelope are close relatives of cows and goats. The even-toed, hoofed mammals spend their days grazing on herbs, grass, and leaves. An antelope's stomach is divided into four compartments, making it easier to digest a plant-based diet. It is believed that antelope get their name from the Greek words *anthos* and *ops*, which translate to "flower eyes." This probably refers to the antelope's big, beautiful eyes and long eyelashes. Antelope have horns they can use to defend themselves. The horns can grow over 3 feet (1 meter) long!

FANCY DRESSERS

There are more than 90 different species of antelope. Their horns come in many different shapes and sizes.

Sable

Tsessebe

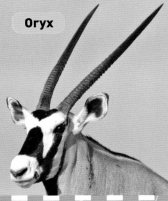
Oryx

Kudu

FUN FACT!

Antelope communicate using a variety of sounds—and scents. Antelope herds leave a trail of scent tracks. If one antelope is separated from the others, it can follow these tracks to find the herd.

FUN FACT!

The name wildebeest is Dutch for "wild beast." If that's too long, you can just call them gnus (pronounced like the word "news"). That name comes from an African word that mimics the grunting sound wildebeests make!

DANGEROUS TRAVELS

The annual wildebeest migration is no walk in the park. The big cats, hyenas, and killer crocodiles have their pick of any animal that gets separated from the pack or becomes too weak to keep up. Each year, about 250,000 wildebeests and 30,000 zebras are killed, or die from exhaustion or dehydration, during migration.

A GREAT MIGRATION

Not all African animals are enemies. Wildebeests and zebras migrate together each year. Zebras lead the way every June, moving slowly and followed closely by the wildebeests.

Wildebeests

ANIMALS ON THE MOVE

A member of the antelope family, the wildebeest doesn't like to keep still. Depending upon the yearly rainfall and availability of food, 1.5 million wildebeests migrate about 1,200 miles (1,930 kilometers) each year from Africa's Serengeti to the Maasai Mara and back. How do wildebeests know when it's time to get moving? Scientists believe herds possess something called swarm intelligence, an instinct that tells them, "You know what? It's moving day!"

BABY BOOM

Between January and March, a whopping 500,000 wildebeests are born in the Serengeti.

Black Rhinoceros

The world's second largest land mammal, the white rhinoceros is huge, weighing up to 8,000 pounds (3,630 kilograms). Despite the name, it's not exactly white, more like a light shade of gray. Rhinos are herbivores and spend almost every minute of the day foraging for plants and leaves. They spend the rest of the day napping and taking mud baths to keep off flies and block the sun.

RHINOCEROSES COME IN 5 DIFFERENT MODELS:

Indian Rhinoceros

- Black rhinoceroses are native to eastern and southern Africa. They are endangered. Poachers hunt and kill them, and there are only about 5,500 left.
- White rhinoceroses are native to South Africa, Namibia, Zimbabwe, and Kenya.
- Indian rhinoceroses are native to India. Today around 3,500 survive.
- Javan rhinoceroses are native to Indonesia, and only 60 remain in the wild.
- Sumatran rhinoceroses are native to Sumatra and Borneo. They are still alive but struggling for survival, with only around 100 left.

Rhinos

THICK-SKINNED, SHORTSIGHTED, AND READY TO CHARGE!

RHINO HORNS

Sadly, one reason rhinoceroses are endangered is because their horns are valued by humans. Made from a protein called keratin, the same substance in human fingernails and hair, rhino horns are in high demand as trophies. They are also used in traditional Asian medicine.

It may look like this hippo is yawning, but when a hippo stretches its mouth wide open—look out! It's a threat gesture. The hippo is showing off its long, thick tusks that are so sharp they can bite a small boat in half!

Hippos

MAKING A **BIG SPLASH**

Hippos live the life! Every day, these supersized natives of Africa chill out in the water, covered in mud to fend off flies and the sun. At night, when it's cool, they lumber to the grasslands to chow down on up to 90 pounds (41 kilograms) of grass and leaves. By sunrise they are back at the pond or waterhole, getting ready to soak for another day. Though hippos might look lumbering and slow, don't be fooled. When angry, a hippo can charge in short bursts of up to 19 miles (30 kilometers) an hour! That's incredibly fast for an animal that can weigh up to five tons (4.5 metric tons)! Even though they are herbivores, hippos can be very aggressive when defending their territory. They attack and kill crocodiles, and they are responsible for more human deaths in Africa than any other large animal.

HIP HIP **HURRAY!**

- The name hippopotamus means "river horse."
- Spending the day in water helps the hippo keep its body temperature low.
- The hippo's closest biological relatives are whales and dolphins.
- Hippos can easily outrun a human.
- A female hippo is called a cow. A group of hippos is called a herd, a pod, a dale, or a bloat.

FUN **FACT!**

The hippo's nose, ears, and eyes are at the top of its head. This way a hippo can breathe, see, and hear while swimming. And hippos love to swim! They are able to hold their breath for up to five minutes—long enough to take a stroll along the bottom of rivers or lakes.

The Circle of Life

EVERYONE PLAYS THEIR PART!

Hyena
predator/scavenger

Antelope
prey

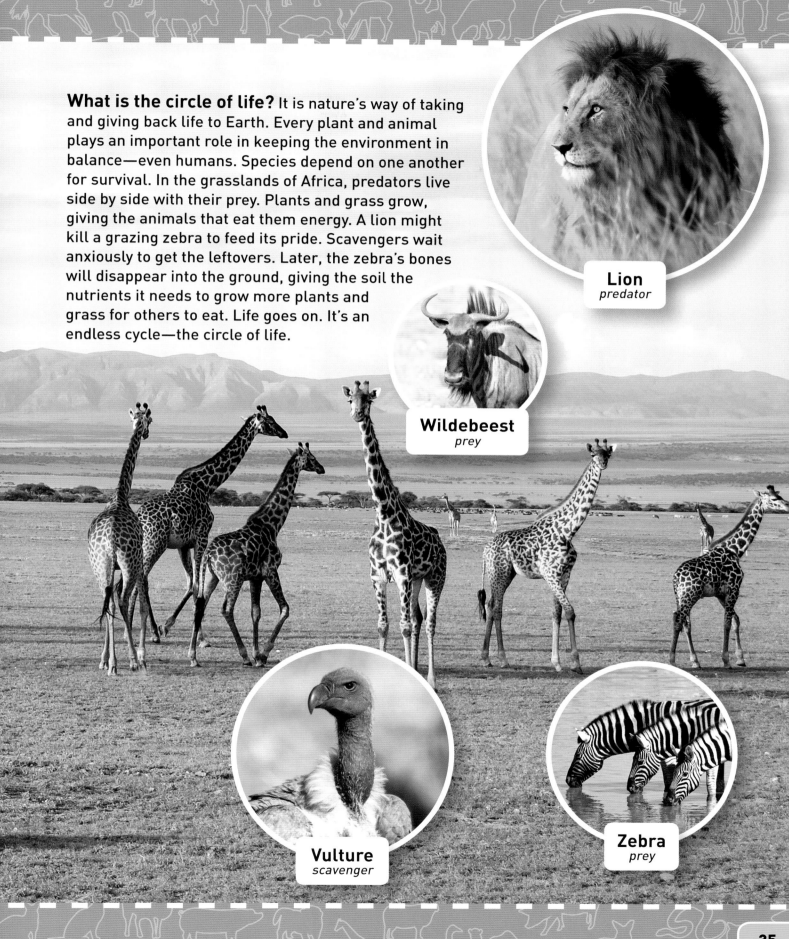

What is the circle of life? It is nature's way of taking and giving back life to Earth. Every plant and animal plays an important role in keeping the environment in balance—even humans. Species depend on one another for survival. In the grasslands of Africa, predators live side by side with their prey. Plants and grass grow, giving the animals that eat them energy. A lion might kill a grazing zebra to feed its pride. Scavengers wait anxiously to get the leftovers. Later, the zebra's bones will disappear into the ground, giving the soil the nutrients it needs to grow more plants and grass for others to eat. Life goes on. It's an endless cycle—the circle of life.

Lion
predator

Wildebeest
prey

Vulture
scavenger

Zebra
prey

More African Animals

CREATURES OF THE CONTINENT

Sure, Africa is home to some of the most celebrated animals in the world. You'll find elephants, lions, giraffes, zebras, and antelopes on the savanna. But alongside these rock stars are some lesser-known animals trying to get a little love. Here's a look at some of Africa's most interesting, not to mention cutest, animals.

The **pangolin** gets its name from a Malay word that means "rolling up." The only mammal in the world that is covered in scales, the pangolin rolls into a tight ball when threatened. Even a lion can't bite through the pangolin's tough scales! With a tongue longer than its entire body, a pangolin can slurp up to 20,000 ants a day.

The **elephant shrew** likes to use its long back legs to hop like a rabbit, earning it the nickname "jumping shrew." There are 20 different species in Africa, and all live exclusively on insects.

A **dwarf mongoose** may look harmless, but these little animals are meat eaters and do a good job hunting and eating the local rat populations.

Galagos (or bush babies) are one of the smallest primates in the world. About the size of a squirrel, a bush baby has large, round eyes for good night vision and bat-like ears that help it stalk prey at night.

They look a bit like pigs, have ears like a rabbit, and kangaroo-like tails, but **aardvarks** aren't related to any of these animals. Their closest biological cousin is the elephant!

Named for its large ears, the **bat-eared fox** uses them to listen for crawling insects. Its tiny mouth is jammed with up to 50 sharp teeth, perfect for munching on its favorite food—termites!

Extinct Animals

BLAST FROM THE PAST

Woolly mammoths are relatives of today's elephants. Standing up to 13 feet (4 meters) tall and weighing in at up to six tons (5.4 metric tons), mammoths lived during the Ice Age that ended about 11,700 years ago. They became extinct as the weather grew warmer. Mammoths had very long tusks, up to 15 feet (4.6 meters) long, which they used for fighting and digging for food in the snow. Herbivores, mammoths ate grass, plants, and flowers.

The **dodo** is a bird that went extinct over 300 years ago. A relative of the pigeon, the dodo evolved over hundreds of thousands of years into a flightless, 40-pound (18-kilogram) bird that stood 3 feet (0.9 meters) tall and lived on the island of Mauritius in Africa. First seen by Dutch settlers in 1598, it took less than 75 years for the dodo to disappear. What happened? Until the arrival of humans, the dodo had absolutely no natural predators. Then humans not only hunted the trusting birds, they destroyed their habitat and introduced animals that competed for the dodo's food sources.

A New Woolly Mammoth?

Because the woolly mammoth lived in the Arctic, their fossils are well preserved.

Perhaps the best specimen belonged to a female mammoth nicknamed Buttercup that lived 40,000 years ago. In theory, some scientists believe that Buttercup's DNA could be used to clone her, bringing an extinct species back to life! But even if that were possible, other scientists point out that the mammoth's habitat isn't what it was when the creature first roamed the Earth. What do you think? Could a mammoth clone survive today?

GONE BUT NOT **FORGOTTEN**

Sometimes called the saber-toothed tiger, Smilodon was a type of saber-toothed cat that roamed North and South America over 10,000 years ago. Although not actually a close relative of modern tigers, these ferocious beasts did make life miserable for the buffalo and deer of the day. While Smilodons lived at the same time as humans, the big cats didn't survive as well as we did. The saber-toothed cats became extinct around the end of the Ice Age.

The Wonders of Madagascar
ISLAND OF AWESOME ANIMALS

Madagascar, an island off the east coast of Africa, holds a unique place in the animal kingdom. It is the habitat of hundreds of species of animals that are found nowhere else in the world. Madagascar is home to over 100 species of lemur, over 260 species of birds, almost 300 types of frogs, over 300 kinds of reptiles, and more. The island is literally teeming with life.

The largest carnivore and top predator on the island, **fossas** eat lemurs, birds, frogs, and insects.

Red-ruffed lemurs are important to the plants of the island. When they stick their long noses deep into flowers to slurp up nectar, they pick up pollen, which they bring to other flowers. This helps more plants grow!

Aye-ayes spend most of their lives in the trees of the rain forest. They use their long middle finger to tap trees and listen for insects to eat.

Lemurs communicate using sounds and scents. **Ring-tailed lemurs** make a cat-like mewing sound to show friendliness. The males fight with stink bombs. They rub their scent glands on their tails and then wave them in each other's faces.

When faced with danger, a **tomato frog** will puff up its body to make itself look larger than it really is.

The lowland streaked **tenrec** looks like a cross between a hedgehog and a bee. Its black and yellow bristles are good camouflage on the rain forest floor.

There are about 200 different species of chameleons in the world, and almost half of them are found on Madagascar. The **panther chameleon** is one of the most colorful species and, like a monkey, it can use its prehensile tail to hang from tree branches.

Animals of the Rain Forest

SOME OF EARTH'S MOST AWESOME TREASURES

The Amazon rain forest is the largest tropical forest on Earth and home to over 400 types of mammals, around 1,300 species of birds, almost 400 varieties of reptiles, and around 400 kinds of amphibians. Rich in animal life, the Amazon rain forest is sometimes called "the lungs of the planet" because its plants produce more than 20 percent of the world's oxygen. All told, there are almost six million species of plant and animal life that call the rain forest home. Here's a look at some of them.

Harpy Eagle

Capybara

Poison Dart Frog

Toucan

Blue Morpho Butterfly

Ocelot

Spider Monkey

Armadillo

Giant Anteater

Golden Lion Tamarin

Arctic Animals

THESE GUYS LOVE THE COLD!

Some animals have evolved to love the cold weather of the Arctic. You've probably heard of one of them, and you might have even sung about them. They're reindeer and their antlered Arctic cousins, caribou!

Caribou and reindeer belong to the same species, but there are differences between them. While the reindeer found in the northern regions of Europe and Asia were domesticated by humans thousands of years ago, the caribou of northern North America and Greenland are wild. Each spring, caribou herds head north, traveling more than 600 miles (965 kilometers) in search of the grasses and plants of the Arctic tundra.

FREEZED TO MEET YOU!

Here are a few other animals that thrive in the Arctic.

Arctic Fox

Muskox

Seal

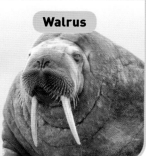
Walrus

Caribou are the only species of deer in which both males and females have antlers.

HOOF **POWER**

Caribou use their large hooves to help them in the cold climate. Here's how:

- The hooves are big enough to support their weight in the snow.
- The large hooves help them paddle through the water.
- The sharp edges of the hooves help the animal grip the ice.
- The underside of the hoof is hollow so that the caribou can use it to dig through snow in search of food.

Polar Bears

CUTE AND CUDDLY . . . AND FEROCIOUS!

Polar bears live in countries that ring the Arctic Circle: Canada, Russia, the United States (in Alaska), Greenland, and Norway. The largest species of bear, polar bears stand as tall as 10 feet (3 meters) on their hind legs. Male bears can weigh in the range of 1,000 pounds (454 kilograms). Though their furry faces may make them look gentle, don't be fooled. Polar bears are considered to be one of the most dangerous carnivores among land animals.

FUN FACT!

The polar bear's scientific name is *Ursus maritimus*, which means "sea bear." Polar bears are excellent swimmers and have swum more than 96 miles (154 kilometers) without rest. Usual swims are around 30 miles (48 kilometers).

Polar bears don't really have white fur. It's actually see-through, and each strand is hollow. The fur only appears white because of the way the light bounces through the bear's clear hair.

SEAL, PLEASE

While all other species of bear hibernate in the winter, polar bears stay out in the cold, continuing to eat year-round. The polar bear will spend days sitting on the ice shelf next to a seal breathing hole, waiting for a seal to appear. This kind of patient hunting is called "still hunting." If there are no seals to be found, a polar bear will eat pretty much anything it can find, including other kinds of small animals, fish, and even human garbage.

WOLF **PACK**

Wolves are the largest members of the dog family, and they live in groups called packs. Each pack is led by the mother and father (called the alphas) and their children. The alphas are the pack leaders who track and lead attacks on prey. Wolves like to eat large animals such as deer and elk, but will settle for rabbits and other smaller game.

Coyotes are also members of the dog family, and they live in North America and Central America. Puppies are born blind and are helpless for the first few weeks of life. Coyotes hunt alone or in pairs, and, though they love to eat big game, they will settle for smaller animals, reptiles, grass, and even garbage. As human populations have grown, coyotes have adapted to city life. Today, coyotes are occasionally even seen in large cities like Los Angeles and New York.

Arctic Wolf

Coyote

WOLVES OR **COYOTES?**

WOLVES	COYOTES
• Broad face with large nose pad	• Narrow, pointed face with small nose pad
• Short, rounded ears	• Tall, pointed ears
• Large, bulky bodies weighing 50 to 100 lbs (23 to 46 kg)	• Shorter, lighter bodies weighing 25 to 45 lbs (11 to 20 kg)
• Long legs and large paws	• Shorter legs and smaller paws

Wolves

ANSWER THE CALL OF THE WILD

The howl of the wolf is a haunting sound—a part of legends and fairy tales. But wolves are not the villains stories have made them out to be. They howl to keep their pack together. When a wolf is out hunting for food, the sound of its howl travels far across the land, letting the others know where it is.

Many years ago, wolves thrived throughout the U.S., and their packs roamed freely. When they began to hunt and eat livestock, farmers used guns and traps to protect their animals from frequent wolf attacks. By the 1930s, wolves were wiped out in much of the country. The loss of wolves had negative effects, though. In Yellowstone National Park, for example, the elk population grew too large without its natural predator. Elk then ate up all the young willow trees. Beaver colonies that needed the willows to survive began to disappear, too. In 1995, wolf packs were reintroduced to the park. Now there are more than 100 wolves there. They are controlling the elk population, so more willows are growing, and the number of beaver colonies is increasing again.

THE **KANGAROO**

Australia is home to over 30 million kangaroos. They are marsupials—mammals that carry their young in a pouch. With strong hind legs and short arms, kangaroos don't walk—they jump!

- There are four types of kangaroo: red, eastern gray, western gray, and antilopine.
- Kangaroos come from an animal family known as macropods, which means "big foot."
- Kangaroos stand between 5 and 6 ft (1.5 and 1.8 m) tall and weigh up to 200 lbs (91 kg).
- A mother kangaroo usually only has one joey, or baby, in her pouch at a time.

Eastern Gray Kangaroo

Animals of Australia

WELCOME TO THE LAND DOWN UNDER!

Australia is a continent filled with a wide range of habitats, from reefs to rain forests, and a wide range of animals, too. Most, nearly 90 percent, are unique to the continent because of its location far away from other landmasses. Marsupials like the kangaroo, wombat, and Tasmanian devil are mammals whose young are raised in pouches. Monotremes like the platypus are mammals that lay eggs. Monotremes aren't found anywhere else on the planet!

Tasmanian Devil

Dingo

Koala

Platypus

Wombat

Blue-tongued Skink

Budgerigar

RED PANDAS!

Even though they share the panda name, red pandas, found in mountain forests of Asia, are not related to giant pandas.

Pandas

UN-BEAR-ABLY CUTE

Giant pandas are one of China's national treasures. Noted for looking like adorable giant stuffed animals, pandas are part of the bear family and stand 4 to 5 feet (1.5 meters) tall and weigh up to 300 pounds (136 kilograms). Pandas like to live in the remote mountains of central China, where there is plenty of bamboo for them to eat. Though pandas are admired worldwide, their survival on the planet is threatened. Only about 1,900 giant pandas live in the wild, with 300 more in zoos around the world.

LEAVE ME ALONE

Though they may be more sociable than once believed, pandas like to spend time alone. In the wild, the panda makes its home in heavily forested areas that are difficult to travel through. Pandas rest during the day in caves, hollowed trees, or thick brush and become active at sunset. A male panda will secrete a dark, sticky substance on rocks and trees to attract a mate as well as to mark its territory so that other male pandas know to stay away.

TASTES GOOD, BUT HARD TO DIGEST

Pandas love bamboo! Left alone, a panda will eat bamboo for 12 hours a day. The panda's stomach is covered with mucus to prevent its lining from being punctured by bamboo splinters. It is also extra muscular to digest all of that tough fiber. Pandas poop up to 40 times a day because of the large quantity of bamboo they eat.

Relatives of anteaters, there are six species of sloths. Until about 10,000 years ago there was also a giant sloth species that weighed up to four tons (3.6 metric tons) and was nearly as big as an elephant!

Sloths
SLOW, SLOWER, **SLOWEST**

ARE SLOTHS REALLY SLOTHFUL?

Are sloths getting a bad rap? Sloths have a reputation for being lazy. It's true that in captivity a sloth sleeps 15 to 20 hours a day. But in the wild, recent studies show that a sloth sleeps a more normal nine or 10 hours.

A sloth is a slow-moving animal native to South and Central America. Solitary creatures, sloths live in trees and move at a rate of about 40 yards (37 meters) a day. That's like taking all day to walk across a soccer field— and only getting partway! Amazingly, because they move so slowly, a sloth's fur can sometimes provide a home to moths, fungi, algae, cockroaches, and beetles.

- Sloths are clumsy on land but are great swimmers.
- Sloths are arboreal creatures. That means that they spend most of their time in trees.
- The algae that can grow on their fur provides them with green camouflage.
- Sloths' primary predators are eagles, snakes, and jaguars.
- A three-toed sloth can turn its head about 270 degrees—that's almost all the way around!
- Sloths can live to age 40.

DEATH GRIP

Sloths have long claws and grip trees very tightly—so tightly that some keep holding on even after they have died, locked in the exact same position they were in when they were alive.

LET'S FAWN OVER...

Deer and Elk

Deer are forest dwellers, known for their shy nature and speedy getaways. There are over 40 species of deer in the world, including caribou, elk, and moose. In America, the white-tailed deer's population has grown so much that they've been seen wandering out of the woods and into backyards.

White-tailed Deer

FAMILY LIFE

A male deer is called a buck, a female is a doe, and a young deer is a fawn. A doe lives alone, except when taking care of fawns. It takes a newborn about 20 minutes to stand. In just five days, it can run fast! Most fawns are born with white spots on their fur that they lose within a year.

ALL ABOUT ANTLERS

- All male deer have antlers, except for the Chinese water deer. Female caribou have antlers, too!
- Every year, a buck's antlers fall off, and then a new rack grows back.
- During mating season, bucks use their antlers to fight for mates.

WHAT A DEER!

The Irish elk was the world's largest deer before it went extinct 11,000 years ago. It's worth remembering. The Irish elk measured 7 feet (2 meters) from hooves to shoulder. Its antlers spread out up to 12 feet (4 meters)!

CALL OF THE WILD

Elk are one of the largest deer species in the world. Male elk make a noise called a bugle that can carry for miles. They use it to announce themselves, challenge other males, and attract females.

PLURAL ANIMALS

Some animal names are the same in the singular as the plural. Just as you might write about a sea full of *fish* (not *fishes*), you would refer to a forest full of *moose* (not *mooses*—and definitely not *meese*!).

Moose

KING OF THE DEER

Moose are enormous. The largest of the deer family, a full-grown moose can weigh up to 1,800 pounds (816 kilograms) and stand 5 to 6.5 feet (1.5 to 1.8 meters) from hooves to shoulders. In keeping with their size, moose have gigantic appetites. During summer, a moose can eat up to 70 pounds (32 kilograms) of shrubs, woody plants, and vegetation a day. Even though the moose is big and powerful, it still has predators to worry about. Moose need to keep an especially sharp lookout for bears, wolf packs, and humans.

WATCH OUT

Moose are so large they have been known to wreck a car if an unsuspecting driver accidentally crashes into one standing in the road. If you are driving in moose territory, steer clear!

ANTLERS

Every spring, male moose grow a new set of antlers. In the fall, as the moose look to mate, they show off their antlers, using them to scare rivals from their territory. As winter approaches, the moose shed their antlers, which is probably a relief. At 40 pounds (18 kilograms), full-grown antlers are heavy to carry around. Luckily, moose have exceptionally strong necks that enable them to lug around the extra weight.

Bears HUGE PAWS AND CLAWS!

They may look as cute as a stuffed teddy bear, but bears in the wild are definitely not cuddly. Found all over the world, bears are dangerous, some species more than others. They are surprisingly fast for their size, strong swimmers, and they are able to climb trees. Bears are pretty shy and are not natural predators of humans. However, bears that have been around human food or garbage can become dangerous to people.

Grizzly Bears

After the polar bear, the grizzly, a subspecies of brown bear, is probably the most feared bear. That's because grizzlies are huge. Most weigh between 300 and 800 pounds (136 and 363 kilograms). Standing on its back feet, a grizzly is between 6 and 8 feet (2 and 2.4 meters) tall.

- Though grizzly bears have brown fur, their shoulder and back hair have white tips, giving them the "grizzled" look that they are named for.
- Grizzly bears are omnivores, meaning that they eat both plants and meat. Seventy-five percent of their diet is composed of berries, leaves, and nuts.
- Grizzlies hibernate for five to eight months, during which time their heart rate slows down and they survive on reserves of fat.
- Grizzly cubs stay with their mother for two to four years. Don't get too close. There are a few things more ferocious than a grizzly protecting her cubs!

WORLD TRAVELERS

Bears are able to adapt to the woods, the mountains, and even the desert. Brown bears are the most well-traveled bear species, having made homes in lands as diverse as northwestern North America, northwestern Africa, northern Asia, and the Middle East. Brown bears that reside in Alaska are called Kodiak or Alaskan brown bears. American black bears live in North America and spectacled bears are found in South America. The Asiatic black bear is sprinkled throughout Asia, and the sloth bear is found in India, Nepal, Bhutan, and Sri Lanka. Polar bears like the cold Arctic, and giant pandas live in China.

EIGHT KINDS OF BEARS

American Black Bear

Sun Bear

Sloth Bear

Spectacled Bear

Polar Bear

Giant Panda Bear

Brown Bear

Asiatic Black Bear

Buffalo
ROLLING THUNDER
Stampede

Call them bison or buffalo, it doesn't matter. By either name, they're pretty impressive. Weighing up to a ton (0.9 metric tons), the American bison is the largest land animal in North America, and the European bison is the largest land animal in—you guessed it—Europe!

Once, the Great Plains of the U.S. were covered with millions of bison. The enormous grazing beasts played a role in shaping the land, munching on grasses, and stirring up the soil as they thundered across it. This helped many plant and animal species thrive. As European settlers moved west, they killed bison to make room for their farms. Railroads cut through the bison territory. Hunters shot the bison for sport and to sell their hides. By the end of the 19th century, the bison were nearly extinct, with only a few hundred left in North America. Still, in the days when the buffalo ruled the west, they were known to stampede. And boy could they run! The stampede is a bison's defense from predators like wolves and grizzly bears. Stampeding buffalo can run at speeds over 30 miles (48 kilometers) per hour and can destroy everything in their path.

TAKE A CLOSER LOOK Small Animals of the Woodlands

A **flying squirrel** glides through the air.

An **otter** swims speedily underwater.

A **skunk** sprays a foul-smelling substance.

A **marmot** stays perfectly still and quiet.

Earth's forests and woodlands, areas covered with lots of trees and plant life, are filled with small mammals. Not big or powerful, each species has developed its own way to protect themselves from predators.

A **rabbit** scurries into underground burrows.

A **beaver** uses its sharp claws and teeth.

An **opossum** gives the appearance of being dead.

A **chipmunk** uses chirps to warn others of danger.

A **mole** lives deep underground.

A **porcupine** has quills that easily detach.

Life on the Farm

BARNYARD BUDDIES

Humans have been farming the land for more than 12,000 years. Farmers have to work hard, but their jobs became a lot easier around 10,000 years ago, when they started raising animals for milk and food. Around 6,000 years ago, they started training animals, such as horses, to help with farm work. Cows, sheep, chickens, goats, pigs, and other animals all became an important part of farm life.

- There are more sheep than people in New Zealand. The island nation has about seven sheep for every human.

- Herding dog breeds like border collies are born with an instinct to round up animals. They stalk, run, nudge, and nip to chase and group a herd. They even give "the eye" by staring at an animal, the way your mom might look at you when she doesn't want you to do something.

- A farmer can tell his pigs' mood by looking at their tails. Curly tails mean happy pigs. Tails tucked between their legs mean the pigs are stressed.

Cows

Sheep

Chickens

FUN FACTS!

- Farming is a family business in the U.S. About 97 percent of U.S. farms are family-owned.

- Instead of a lawn mower, a flock of sheep kept the White House lawn neat and trimmed during World War I.

- Goats are incredibly curious. Always looking for an escape route, they'll hop on the backs of bigger animals to jump over fences to see what is on the other side.

- Pigs are so smart that researchers have been able to teach them how to play simple video games. The pigs used a joystick to hit targets on a screen.

- The average dairy cow produces seven gallons (26 liters) of milk every day.

- On a farm, draft animals are the ones that work to pull heavy loads. Horses, donkeys, and cattle are popular draft animals in the U.S.; in South America, llamas are.

Goats

Pigs

Horses

MOOOOVE OVER FOR . . .
COWS

Cows have provided people with milk and meat for more than 10,000 years. Today, there are over 800 breeds of cattle (or cows) and over one billion cows in the world. If you'd like to raise a cow, you'd better be prepared to feed it! Cows eat around 50 pounds (22 kilograms) of food a day and wash it down with 35 gallons (132 liters) of water!

FUN FACT!

It takes 350 squirts from a cow's udder to get 1 gallon (3.7 liters) of milk.

THE SACRED ANIMAL

About 80 percent of the people living in India practice Hinduism, a religion which, among other things, respects and honors cows. In India, cows roam the streets freely. Killing or eating a cow is illegal in most of India, but you can drink all the cow milk you want! India is actually the world's largest producer and consumer of milk.

DID YOU KNOW?

Cows are emotional creatures. They have been known to produce more milk when they are treated kindly. Cows also form close friendships (much like humans) and prefer to spend most of their time with two to four friends. Cows are good parents, too. Mother cows have been known to walk for miles to find a lost calf.

DO COWS REALLY HAVE FOUR STOMACHS?

Cows are ruminants. That means they have one stomach that is divided into four chambers called the rumen, reticulum, omasum, and abomasum. These chambers help cows better digest the grass and other plants they eat.

Horses

GIDDYUP!

Dogs may be known as "man's best friend," but horses have had a close relationship with people for thousands of years, too. Scientists believe horses have lived on Earth for about 55 million years. They were first domesticated, or tamed, in Asia 5,000 to 6,000 years ago. At first, horses were used for milk and meat. Soon they joined oxen as a form of transportation. Today there are over 350 different breeds of horses that can be found in all parts of the world, with the exception of Antarctica.

FUN FACTS!

- Horses can sleep both standing up and lying down.
- Horses have 205 bones.
- An average horse gallops at about 27 mph (43 kph).
- Horses live in groups called herds.
- Horses in North America evolved from early dog-size, horse-like animals that were less than 3 ft (0.9 m) tall and weighed about 20 lbs (9 kg).

GRAZING ALL DAY

Though they love to eat grass, domesticated horses are also fed grains like oats, corn, barley, and wheat. Many owners also give their horses salt blocks to lick. Horses have relatively small stomachs for their body size. Because they can't handle large amounts of food at one time, they have to graze throughout the day to get the food they need to keep going.

PONY RIDE

Although they share a family tree and look a lot alike, ponies and horses are actually different animals. So how can you tell them apart?

- Size is the main difference between ponies and horses. Ponies are much smaller.
- Ponies have thicker manes and tails than horses.
- Ponies have shorter legs, thicker necks, and shorter heads than horses.
- Shetland ponies are especially small but very strong. Pound for pound, ponies are stronger than horses.

MORGANS, THOROUGHBREDS, AND MUSTANGS
Horse Breeds

Some types of horses are more well-known than others. Here is a closer look at some of the most famous horse breeds.

A Thoroughbred

The Thoroughbred line can be traced back to 17th- and 18th-century Britain and three Arabian stallions. Their need for speed is in their DNA! Thoroughbreds are extremely athletic, sleek, and fast. They have very long legs, which make them ideal racehorses and show horses.

The Morgan Horse

The Morgan horse can trace its lineage back to a single animal. Figure, born in 1789, was an impressive specimen. Compact and muscular, he could outwalk, outrun, and outpull other horses in the area. His owner was a teacher and businessman named Justin Morgan. Soon, stories began to spread about the "Justin Morgan horse," and other horse farmers wanted Figure to breed with their females. Today, the Morgan horse is the state animal of Vermont. A sturdy breed, Morgan horses are known for their good nature, strength, and intelligence.

Wild Horses:
The Mustang

Wild mustangs are descendants of Spanish horses brought to the Americas in the 16th century. Their name comes from the Spanish word *mestengo*, meaning "a wild or stray animal." Today, mustangs live in the western United States under the protection of the American government. Mustangs live in large herds. Each herd consists of one stallion, about eight females, and their offspring. Most of their day is spent grazing peacefully, but if danger is near, the mares will lead the herd to safety while the stallion stays to fight.

Sheep

I WOOLLY LOVE EWE

A LONG HISTORY OF WOOL

There is historical evidence that wool cloth from sheep existed as far back as 10,000 BCE. Historians also believe that by 55 BCE, British woolen clothes were prized around the world, suggesting that a thriving wool industry had already developed in the nation.

THE BACHELOR

Sheep live in herds, but their herds are a little different from those of other animals. Sheep divide into groups according to their gender. Male sheep in the wild (called rams) live in bachelor herds of 5 to 50 animals. The females (or ewes) live in nursery herds of 5 to 100 animals that also include their offspring. Male sheep fight for dominance in their groups by backing up, running full speed ahead, and ramming horns. These battles can sometimes last for hours. The sheep that doesn't give up wins.

There are five species of wild sheep, including the bighorn of America's Rocky Mountains. Sheep are related to antelope, cattle, muskoxen, and goats, and like these animals, they are ruminants. They have cloven hooves, which means the hooves are split in two. Among the first animals to be tamed by humans, sheep are raised all over the world for their wool, milk, and meat.

WHAT'S IN A CUD?

Sheep are herbivores, and to help digest their food, they swallow a steady diet of seeds, grass, and plants. They chew, swallow, and then regurgitate, or spit it up, back into their mouths. Does that sound gross? Well, it gets worse. After that, the sheep re-chew the food and swallow it again. This regurgitated food is called cud.

CAFFEINATED GOATS?

According to popular legend, coffee was first discovered by goat herders. The herders noticed something interesting: Their goats had a lot more energy after eating coffee beans.

FUN FACTS!

- There are over 450 million goats in the world.
- Goats were brought to the Americas by Christopher Columbus.
- Both male and female goats can grow a beard.
- Like dogs, goats can be taught to come when their name is called.
- Some people use goats as natural lawn mowers.

GOT MILK?

It wasn't a cow that was first domesticated for its milk. It was a goat. Ancient people in the Middle East first sampled goat milk more than 10,000 years ago.

Goats

JUST KIDDING AROUND

Goats have become true Internet animal celebrities. Screaming goats, fainting goats, and goats rushing down hills can all be found in viral videos that entertain millions of people. Those celebrity goats are domestic goats, a type of goat that is usually found on farms and not in front of a camera. Wild goat species include the ibex, found in Eurasia and Africa. Wild goats can climb trees and balance on a ledge nearly as thin as a tightrope. Goats have horns made of keratin, and most young goats, called kids, are born with horn buds. These tiny bumps will develop into horns that will keep growing throughout a goat's life. You can actually tell a goat's age by counting the growth rings on its horns.

DID YOU **KNOW?**

While mountain goats like company in the winter, they prefer to keep to themselves in the summer. Male mountain goats sometimes live by themselves year-round, only returning to the herd during mating season.

DID YOU KNOW?

- Llamas are large. They can reach 6 ft (2 m) tall and weigh up to 500 lbs (227 kg).
- A llama's body is covered with wool.
- Llamas are often divided into 2 groups according to the length of their fur: short-coated and medium-coated.
- A llama has a long face, large nostrils, and long ears that are curved inward.
- Llamas are herbivores, or plant-eaters.
- A llama is not hoofed. It has 2 toenails on each foot and a leathery pad underneath.
- A llama's average life span is 20 years (or longer in captivity).

HUM A HAPPY SONG

Llamas like to hang out with other llamas and with grazing cattle. Llamas are very curious and will sometimes walk right up to a human. They communicate their various moods with a series of tail, body, and ear movements. Many llamas hum when they are happy! On the other hand, a frightened or worried llama will let out a shrill yell.

PACK ME UP

A llama can carry lots of weight. The people of the Andes Mountains have used the llama as a pack animal for centuries. A typical load might weigh between 50 and 75 pounds (23 and 34 kilograms). A llama can carry this weight up to 20 miles (32 kilometers), even through difficult terrain. A herd of llamas toting goods is called a pack train.

Llamas CAMEL COUSINS

Llamas are part of the camel family. Which means that they come from Africa, right? Wrong! Surprisingly, the first home of the camel was North America. In fact, camels spent 40 million years in what is now the United States before migrating to Africa and Asia around three million years ago. At the same time, llama-like creatures were migrating to South America. Then, four to six thousand years ago, llamas were domesticated in Peru. In the 1800s and early 1900s, animal collectors and zoos reintroduced this wonderful breed to the United States. Today, there are seven million llamas, along with their alpaca cousins, in South America. The United States is home to 135,000 llamas, where they are known for their exceptionally soft wool.

THE SPITTERS

Yes, it's true, llamas spit—usually over a dispute involving food. Thankfully, they generally don't spit at people.

Pigs

A FILTHY ANIMAL . . . NOT!

Pigs have been given a bum rap. After all, most people think pigs are dirty animals. In truth, pigs actually prefer to be clean. The reason they roll in the mud is to cool off. Pigs are also highly intelligent. A newborn pig can recognize its name within two weeks! Mother pigs have been known to sing to their piglets when they are nursing. In fact, pigs are more like humans than you might think. Their genetic makeup is close to our own. As a result, scientists are using stem cells from pigs to try to find cures for human diseases.

DID YOU KNOW?

- Like humans, pigs are omnivores, meaning they eat both meat and plants.
- Pigs have poor eyesight but an excellent sense of smell.
- There are 2 billion pigs in the world.

NOT SO SLOW

Considering their short legs and stocky bodies, pigs are pretty fast. Running at full speed, a pig can motor along at 11 miles (18 kilometers) per hour.

RAVENOUS EATERS

Ever heard the expression "to eat like a pig"? Pigs will eat practically anything. That's why farmers throw all their leftovers in the pig slop, including bones.

CHATTING IT UP

Scientists have discovered over 20 different sounds and vocalizations that pigs use to communicate with one another. All those oinks and squeals may be incomprehensible to us, but to a pig, it is a conversation.

WHAT'S SO BUNNY ABOUT... Rabbits

In the wild, rabbits live in underground burrows that are connected to one another by mazes of tunnels. These little underground societies are called warrens. Rabbit habitats include meadows, woods, forests, grasslands, deserts, and wetlands. More than half the world's rabbit population lives in North America, but wild rabbits can be found pretty much all over the world. Known for their long ears, strong back legs, and impressive hopping ability, rabbits are herbivores that love grass, lettuce, and other greens. Rabbits are crepuscular, which means they sleep most of the day and eat at sunrise and sunset.

DID YOU KNOW?

- A female rabbit is called a doe, a male is a buck, and a young rabbit is a kitten or kit.

- Rabbits live to be about 10 years old in captivity.

- Rabbits reproduce very quickly. This can cause problems for farms next to rabbit warrens. With so many rabbit babies always being born, they are almost impossible to drive away.

- A rabbit's distinctive ears give it impressive hearing. A rabbit can hear clearly in two directions at once.

FUN FACT!

When a rabbit is very happy it jumps in the air, twisting its feet and head. This joyful little dance is called a binky.

RABBIT or HARE?

Rabbits

Hares

RABBITS	HARES
• Born hairless, blind, and completely helpless	• Born with fur, can see, and can live on their own just one hour after being born
• Smaller, chubbier body	• Larger, thinner body with bigger rear legs and paws
• Fur stays same color year-round	• Fur of some species changes color from brown or gray in summer to white in winter
• Shorter ears that slant back	• Longer ears that stick straight up

WHAT'S IN A NAME?

Domestic chickens are called by many different names. Babies are chicks. Female chickens are pullets until they are old enough to lay eggs. That's when they become hens. Male chickens less than a year old are called cockerels. Depending upon where you live, adult male chickens are roosters or cocks.

DID YOU KNOW?

- The chicken is the closet living relative of the *T. rex*.
- A chicken's egg has a yellow yolk that provides all the food a baby chick needs to grow.

HIGH I.Q.

Chickens are able to remember and recognize over 100 individuals, including humans! Unlike human babies, they can also understand that when an object is hidden from them, it still exists.

Chickens

RULING THE ROOST

Did you know that there are over 20 million chickens in the world? A domestic subspecies that was bred from wild jungle fowl, the chicken is a member of the pheasant family. Chickens were probably first domesticated for entertainment purposes, but then kept around for their eggs and meat. Today, there are over 90 chicken breeds, such as the Dutch bantam, leghorn, and Rhode Island red.

TOUGH CHICKENS

In a chicken coop, the more powerful birds, usually male, dominate or control the less powerful by growling and fighting. This is where the term "pecking order" originates.

CHICKEN TALK!

The squawks a chicken makes aren't just for show. Scientists have deduced that those chicken sounds have meaning. Here is a brief look at some chicken vocabulary:

- **Cluck:** The sound a hen makes to her young, saying "stay close."
- **Laying cackle:** The sound made by a hen to celebrate laying a really good egg.
- **Broody growl:** A threatening sound made by a hen, saying, "Get away from my eggs, or else."
- **Roosting call:** A low-pitched, repetitive sound made at nightfall that says, "Here's a good spot to sleep."

Land Birds

THESE GUYS ARE **GROUNDED**

Birds such as ostriches, emus, and penguins have wings and feathers, but not the ability to fly. Scientists agree that they are all descended from birds that could fly, but they disagree about why they aren't able to now. One theory is that after living in areas with no natural predators, they no longer needed the ability to fly away to escape. Another theory is that they evolved to have other strengths that helped them get away from predators, like an ostrich's fast land speed or a penguin's swimming ability.

The **emu** is the largest bird in Australia, and the ostrich (from Africa) is the only taller bird in the world. Emus lay blue-green eggs. The color acts as camouflage.

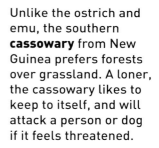

While other cormorants can fly, the **flightless cormorant** from the Galapagos archipelago has wings that are too short and stubby to achieve liftoff. However, this cormorant is a superior diver. It can even reach the ocean floor to feed on fish and plants.

The largest breed of penguin, **the emperor**, lives in Antarctica. Emperor penguins migrate hundreds of miles across the continent every year, walking and swimming to get to their nesting grounds.

Unlike the ostrich and emu, the southern **cassowary** from New Guinea prefers forests over grassland. A loner, the cassowary likes to keep to itself, and will attack a person or dog if it feels threatened.

DID YOU **KNOW?**

- Ostriches have a mean kick and they aren't afraid to use it to defend themselves. Along with being powerful, an ostrich foot has a long claw—their kick can kill a lion or a human.

- Contrary to myth, ostriches do not bury their heads in the sand.

- Due to hunting by people and lions, the wild population of ostriches has decreased in recent years. Today, most ostriches live in game parks.

- Ostriches can go days without drinking water.

Native to Africa, the **ostrich** is the biggest bird in the world. These birds are fast, reaching speeds of up to 40 miles (64 kilometers) per hour.

The **pygmy marmoset** is the world's smallest monkey. It can fit in a teacup!

One of the smallest reptiles in the world, the ***Brookesia minima chameleon*** measures less than 1 inch (2.5 centimeters) long!

DON'T OVERLOOK THE . . .
World's Tiniest Animals

The smallest frog in the world wasn't observed by scientists until 2009. It's such a recent discovery that it only has a scientific name: *Paedophryne amauensis.*

The world is full of beautiful, strange, and glorious animals. Some are very large—here's looking at you, elephant! And some are small—hello, mouse! Some are really, REALLY tiny. Here's a look at some of Mother Nature's tiniest creatures.

Not tipping the scales at only 0.063 ounces (1.8 grams), the **Etruscan shrew** is the smallest mammal by mass.

A Caribbean island is home to the world's smallest snake. The **Barbados threadsnake** is about as wide as a spaghetti strand.

LET'S SPEND A WHILE WITH THE . . . Reptiles

Lizards and snakes and dinosaurs—oh my! So what is a reptile anyway? Reptiles are cold-blooded animals. Unlike mammals or birds, reptiles do not have fur or feathers. Instead, they have dry skin that is often covered with scales or bony plates. They reproduce by laying eggs.

Chameleon

- Crocodiles have been known to swallow rocks to help digest their food. It might even help them dive deeper in the water.
- Some snakes have over 300 pairs of ribs.
- A turtle's shell is made up of 60 interconnected bones.
- Lizards and snakes smell with their tongues!

SUN SOAKERS

Warm-blooded animals, like humans, maintain a steady body temperature. Cold-blooded animals do not. This means that if a reptile gets cold, it has to lie out in the sun to warm up. On the other hand, reptiles don't burn as much energy as mammals do keeping their bodies warm. As a result, they don't have to eat as much food.

TYPES OF **REPTILES**

Reptiles can be found on every continent of the globe, except Antarctica. Some of the most common reptiles are:

Snakes

Crocodiles

Alligators

Turtles

Lizards

Snakes

HISS ME, YOU FOOL!

Python

DID YOU KNOW?

- Snakes don't have eyelids.
- There are around 3,000 different species of snakes in the world.
- Snakes shed their skin a few times a year.
- Some sea snakes can breathe partially through their skin.

Snakes are legless reptiles that slither and hiss. Snakes come in all shapes and sizes, from the world's smallest threadsnake, to the reticulated python, a creature that can grow over 20 feet (6 meters) long! Snakes are carnivores and eat only meat. While some snakes kill their prey with poisonous venom, most snakes smother or squeeze them to death. Constrictors, like anacondas and pythons, seize their prey with their mouths, and then wrap their bodies around their meal. They squeeze tighter and tighter until the prey stops breathing and dies. This is especially impressive because snakes can eat animals 75 to 100 percent of their own body size. There are recorded instances of snakes eating crocodiles and even cows!

Albinos Pacific Gopher Snake

BIG BITES!

Snakes can bite, but they can't chew food, which means they have to swallow everything they eat whole. Luckily, snakes have flexible jaws that allow them to eat prey bigger than their heads!

Eastern Garter Snake

Garter Snake

Corn Snake

There are thousands of kinds of snakes in the world. Most aren't dangerous. Here are some of nature's friendlier snakes.

Black Rat Snake

Northern Water Snake

Emerald Tree Boa

Most Dangerous Snakes

DO NOT TOUCH!

Some snakes are feared by many people, and with good reason. At least 20,000 people around the world die each year from a deadly snakebite. Here are some snakes you definitely want to avoid.

The fierce snake or **inland taipan** possesses the most toxic venom of any land snake in the world. One bite has enough poison to kill about 100 humans. Luckily, this snake likes to keep to itself and is rarely seen in the wild.

A **tiger snake's** bite can paralyze a person in an hour. It's an Australian native.

The **eastern brown snake** of Australia is fast-moving and can be aggressive. Just a tiny drop of its venom is enough to kill a human.

The **rattlesnake**, native to the Americas, is known for its telltale rattle, a warning to those it might strike.

The **blue krait**, native to Southeast Asia and Indonesia, has powerful venom that paralyzes the muscles of its victims.

The **black mamba**, found in Africa, is the fastest land snake in the world, able to slither at speeds of 12 miles (19 kilometers) per hour. The venom of a single black mamba bite could kill anywhere from 10 to 25 humans.

Crocodiles
SNAP TO IT

Cuban Crocodile

Crocodiles are large water-dwelling reptiles. Cold-blooded and unable to regulate their own body temperature, crocs prefer warm climates. There are 14 species of crocodiles. The smallest is the dwarf crocodile, which grows to around 5 feet (1.5 meters). The largest, the saltwater crocodile, is the largest living reptile and can reach 20 feet (6 meters) long. Crocs are carnivores that feast on fish, birds, frogs, and whatever other small animals they can catch in their massive jaws. In the wild, crocodiles can live to be 40 to 70 years old.

RED EYES

Crocodiles have fantastic eyesight that gets even better at night. Unfortunately for crocs, their eyes reflect back light that shines on them, making them easier to spot by hunters.

Freshwater Crocodile

CHEW ON THIS!

On the hunt, crocs catch their prey in their massive jaws, then gulp it down—without chewing! You might wonder why, since crocodiles have at least 60 very sharp teeth. The problem is, crocs can't chew. Their teeth aren't lined up to break up pieces of food. To aid digestion, crocodiles swallow stones. These rocks grind up the food in a crocodile's stomach.

BIG EATERS, BIG NAPPERS

During colder months, crocodiles go dormant, which is almost like hibernating. They burrow into the side of a riverbank, then they take a nice long nap, waiting for warmer weather.

HELLO, MOM!
I'M READY!

Crocodiles usually bury their eggs in the sand. When they are ready to hatch, baby crocs make small noises until their mother hears them. After she digs the eggs up, the mother croc protects the newborns as they hatch. Then she carries them in her mouth to the riverbank to search for food. She stays with them from a few months to a year.

GOLD MEDAL SWIMMERS

American Crocodile

Crocodiles are generally more comfortable in the water than on land. They move a lot faster in water as well. Using their powerful tail, crocs can reach speeds of about 20 miles (32 kilometers) per hour. On land, crocs can sprint for a short time, but they tire out pretty quickly.

WHERE ARE YOU FROM?

There are two types of alligator, American and Chinese. American alligators live in the southern United States and tend to like slow-moving rivers and swamps. They can grow up to 15 feet (5 meters), including their tails, and weigh up to 1,000 pounds (454 kilograms). Chinese alligators are much smaller, measuring four to 5 feet (1.2 to 1.5 meters) and weighing around 50 pounds (23 kilograms). They live in a small area in the Yangtze River basin, which is near the Pacific Ocean. Today, Chinese alligators are endangered because much of their habitat has been converted to rice paddies.

American Alligator

Chinese Alligator

BASKING IN THE SUN

Alligators like company and live in groups called congregations. Being cold-blooded and unable to regulate their body temperature internally, they like to sunbathe when they are cold, and then cool off in the water when they are hot. There they can really move, using their powerful tails to swim as fast as 20 miles (32 kilometers) per hour.

DID YOU KNOW?

- Alligators have been on Earth for millions of years.
- Though alligators have a powerful bite, the muscles that open their jaws are weak. An adult human could hold an alligator's jaw shut with his or her bare hands.
- Alligator eggs become male or female depending upon the temperature where they are nurtured. An egg hatches a male in warmer temperatures and a female when it's cooler.

Alligators
MISTAKEN IDENTITY

Alligators are often mistaken for crocodiles. Although the two reptiles are both members of the order Crocodilia, they are very different. The differences are easy to spot, if you know what to look for. Crocodiles are gray-green, while alligators are charcoal gray to black. Crocs have narrow and pointed noses, and when their mouths are closed, only the fourth tooth on the lower jaw can be seen. Alligators have U-shaped noses, and when an alligator closes its mouth, all its upper teeth are visible. Like crocs, alligators are carnivores. They feed on whatever small prey they can find around the swamp, including fish, rodents, and small mammals.

The **alligator snapping turtle** is the largest freshwater turtle in North America. It lures in fish with its wormlike tongue. Then it snaps its prey with powerful jaws that can bite through fingers, limbs, and organs.

Alligator Snapping Turtle

Turtles

PLAYING THE **SHELL GAME**

Turtles are reptiles with a very distinctive feature—a hard shell that protects them from predators. Generally slow-moving, turtles evolved millions of years ago and are among the oldest reptiles on Earth. Turtles live almost everywhere on the planet except the Arctic and Antarctica. They come in a wide range of sizes. The largest sea turtle is the leatherback. Leatherbacks weigh between 600 and 1,500 pounds (272 and 680 kilograms). The alligator snapping turtle is the largest turtle in North America, growing to 2.5 feet (0.75 meters) and weighing up to 200 pounds (91 kilograms). Other turtles are quite tiny in comparison. The cape tortoise has a shell only about 3 inches (8 centimeters) long. Regardless of their size, turtles are omnivores and eat small fish, plants, and insects.

HOME SWEET SHELL

Like a rabbit's ears or a porcupine's quills, a turtle's shell is its most identifiable feature. The shell itself is made up of about 60 bones that are covered with plates called scutes. These scutes are made of keratin. The top part of the shell is called the carapace and the bottom, the plastron. Many species of turtles have the ability to pull their heads and feet into their shells when a predator is near or when they just want to be left alone.

DID YOU KNOW?

- Turtles have been on Earth for millions of years and evolved before mammals, birds, crocodiles, and snakes.
- Several species of turtles live to be over 100 years old.
- Most turtles have 5 toes on each limb.
- Some aquatic turtles can absorb oxygen through the skin on their necks, allowing them to stay underwater for a very long time.

BARK . . . LIKE A TURTLE?

Turtles can make some pretty strange sounds. Some bark, some belch, and the red-footed tortoise from South America clucks!

TURTLE OR TORTOISE?

TURTLES	TORTOISES
• Spend most of their lives in the water	• Spend most of their lives on land
• Webbed feet	• Round, stumpy feet
• Streamlined bodies	• Large, dome-shaped bodies
• Mostly lightweight shell	• Heavier shell

Hawksbill Turtle

Leopard Tortoise

The **green iguana** is common to Central and South America and can grow to be 6 feet (1.8 meters) long.

Colorful REPTILIAN RAINBOW Lizards

Mother Nature has given the world some pretty gorgeous lizards. Don't look away—reptiles have never looked so good!

The **barking gecko** gets its name because—why else? It barks!

The **Galapagos land iguana** is native to the Galapagos Islands, which are in the Pacific Ocean off the coast of Ecuador.

Most reptiles have green skin to help them blend in with their surroundings, but some are more colorful. Their bright colors evolved over many years, either as a protective device to warn predators to stay away, or as a way of attracting mates.

The **Indo-Chinese forest lizard** lives in Southeast Asia. This lizard often sports red spots on its back.

The **rainbow agama** hails from Africa. During mating season, the male agama explodes with color. Its head and neck turn bright orange and its body becomes dark blue.

The American **five-lined skink**, native to North America, is known for its blue tail and five yellow stripes on its body.

The **gold dust day gecko** from Madagascar and the Comoros changes color from bright green to yellow-green to blue. Its back is covered with yellow speckles. Its upper eyelids, feet, and toes are blue.

Dangerous Lizards

DOCTOR'S WARNING: BE FRIGHTENED!

Some lizards are harmless; some are beautiful. But some are huge, terrifying, and downright dangerous. If you see any of these creatures in the wild, heed this advice: Get away AS FAST AS YOU POSSIBLY CAN!

The **Mexican beaded lizard**, like its relative the Gila monster, is venomous. This lizard locks its jaws on its prey and lets venom seep into the wound.

The **water monitor** is native to Southeast Asia. The second heaviest lizard in the world, weighing up to 100 pounds (45 kilograms), is venomous and has a bite that is powerful enough to crush human bones.

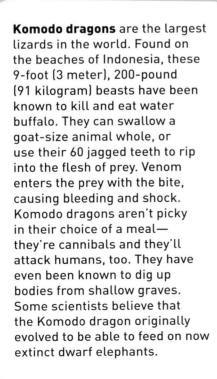

Komodo dragons are the largest lizards in the world. Found on the beaches of Indonesia, these 9-foot (3 meter), 200-pound (91 kilogram) beasts have been known to kill and eat water buffalo. They can swallow a goat-size animal whole, or use their 60 jagged teeth to rip into the flesh of prey. Venom enters the prey with the bite, causing bleeding and shock. Komodo dragons aren't picky in their choice of a meal— they're cannibals and they'll attack humans, too. They have even been known to dig up bodies from shallow graves. Some scientists believe that the Komodo dragon originally evolved to be able to feed on now extinct dwarf elephants.

Not only is the **Gila monster** North America's largest lizard at up to 20 inches (0.5 meters) long, it is also venomous. The Gila monster doesn't have fangs, but holds on extra tight when it bites. This frightening creature has been known to latch onto a human hand and not let go.

Amphibians

ON LAND AND IN WATER

Amphibians are cold-blooded animals with backbones. Though they resemble reptiles, they also possess characteristics of fish. That makes sense, because amphibians are able to spend time on land and in the water. Their larvae, or offspring, grow up in water, breathing through gills like fish. As they mature, they move to the land, breathing through their skin and lungs. There are over 7,700 different species of amphibians, which are divided into three groups: frogs and toads, salamanders and newts, and wormlike creatures called caecilians.

STAY WET!

Like reptiles, amphibians are cold-blooded. Unable to regulate their own body temperature, they take on the temperature of the environment. Their skin needs constant water to stay moist. If it gets too hot, they dry out and die. That's why amphibians like to live near ponds, marshlands, swamps, and lakes.

THE LIFE CYCLE

An amphibian's life begins in water. A female amphibian lays its eggs there and tadpoles hatch from many of the eggs. The tadpoles have dark, oval bodies, tails that help them move through the water, and gills to breathe underwater. As they grow, they go through a process called metamorphosis, which means "a change in physical form." This is the stage when the tadpole changes into an adult amphibian, like a frog or toad. Lungs develop, legs sprout, and the tail grows smaller or disappears. The adult amphibian will spend less time in the water and more time on land.

WHAT IN THE WORLD IS ESTIVATION?

When it's too hot or too dry to survive, some amphibians become inactive. This inactive state is called estivation when it happens during hot temperatures. It's called hibernation when the weather is cold. Estivating amphibians are able to shut down, and then return to normal life when conditions are more favorable.

Ants

SUPER STRENGTH
IN A SMALL PACKAGE

Ants are among the smallest insects in the world, but don't let their size fool you. Ants are typically able to carry between 10 and 50 times their body weight. The Asian weaver ant can carry up to 100 times its weight! Ants are everywhere. Some estimates say that there are one million of the little creatures for every human being. This makes ants one of the great evolutionary success stories. Today, there are more than 10,000 known species of ants in the world.

POWER EATERS

Ants like to eat nectar, seeds, fungus, and other insects. Ants can team up and prey on reptiles, birds, or even small mammals!

WANT TO HANG?

Ants live together in giant colonies numbering in the thousands. These colonies are headed by one or more queens. A queen's sole function in life is to lay lots and lots of eggs. The worker ants, the ones you see on the sidewalk, are females who do not reproduce. Their job is to find food for the colony. A male ant's only job is to mate with the queen. After that, many of them die.

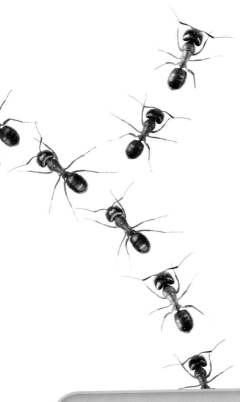

THE ANT'S BODY

- Ants use their antennae to hear, taste, touch, and smell.

- An ant's body is made up of three parts: the head, the trunk (thorax), and the abdomen at the rear.

- Ants don't have a heart. A tube that moves liquids runs through an ant's body from head to abdomen.

- Like all insects, ants have 6 legs that are attached to the thorax.

DID YOU KNOW?

- Ants, like all insects, don't have lungs. They breathe through holes in the sides of their bodies called spiracles.

- Ants don't have ears. They hear by sensing vibrations.

- Ants have two stomachs: one for their own food, the other to store food for friends working back at the colony.

THE ANTHILL

Ants live in colonies. Some make mounds of dirt and twigs, called anthills. Inside each hill is a complex maze of tunnels and passageways that connect to different rooms. Some of these chambers are used to store food, and others are used to care for baby ants.

Spiders
SURFING THE WEB

Spiders are part of the arachnid class, a group of creatures that also includes scorpions and ticks. Spiders are eight-legged and have the unique ability to spin silk out of the ends of their bodies. About half of spider species use the silk to make elaborate and sticky webs to trap food. Once a fly or other insect is caught, the spider holds it in its fangs, injects it with venom, and then has a tasty meal to eat or save for later. Since spider guts are too narrow to take in solids, they liquidize their food by drenching it in digestive enzymes.

SPIN THAT WEB

What makes spider silk so strong? It is filled with strong strands of protein. Individual species of spiders can produce up to seven distinct types of silk. Each type of silk has a special function, from trapping prey to lining burrows. Spiderwebs don't break easily either. By some measurements, the stress a web can withstand before breaking is greater than a human bone and half the strength of steel.

GET THAT THING AWAY FROM ME!

No question about it: Many people find spiders simply terrifying! There is actually a word to describe the fear of spiders. It's arachnophobia. Some biologists have considered the possibility that arachnophobia is a remainder of an instinctive response that helped early humans survive.

SPIDERS RULE

There are over 44,000 species of spiders, and they've been living all over the world (except Antarctica) for a long, long time. Fossilized spiders have been found in rocks dating back 380 million years!

TUMMY TIME

A spider's abdomen is where most of its important internal organs are located, including its reproductive system, lungs, and digestive tract. Also on the abdomen are the spinnerets. They're the silk-producing organs of a spider.

SO MANY EYES, SO LITTLE TO SEE

Spiders can have between zero and 12 eyes. Most have eight. Even so, most spiders can't see more than the difference between light and shadow.

DID YOU KNOW?

- Spiders are arachnids, not insects.
- Spiders have 8 legs. Insects have 6.
- Spiders don't have antennae. Insects do.
- Abandoned spiderwebs are called cobwebs.
- Most spiders are harmless to humans, but a few are venomous, including the black widow. Death from a spider bite is rare, however.
- Tarantulas—large, hairy spiders—have been known to kill mice, lizards, and birds.

Insect Behavior

MYSTERIOUS MANNERS

Most people don't think of insects as being particularly intelligent. After all, what do bugs know? A lot, actually! We already know that insects can demonstrate amazing teamwork, like the ants in a colony or bees in a hive. There are some that behave in ways that seem downright genius!

CATERPILLARS LINE UP

The pine processionary caterpillar lives in pine forests throughout Europe and Asia. This pest has a very organized way of eating, forming lines of hundreds of hungry caterpillars. After they have eaten all they want from one tree, they rest for a day, and then line up again. A scientist once arranged them in a circle, and they kept marching in the circle for a week!

BRILLIANT NAVIGATORS

Ants are able to take the most mathematically logical route to reach a food source. Here's how it works: Every time an ant returns to its colony from a food source, it leaves a trail of pheromone. That's a chemical substance released by the ants into the environment. On trips back to the food, ants are instinctively able to follow the previous ants' pheromone path. Very quickly, multiple trails combine into one master trail—the one that is the most direct route.

ELECTRIC FLOWERS

Flowers have developed signals to lure bees and butterflies to spread their pollen. Bees have the ability to sense the tiny electrical field emitted by a flower. After sensing an individual flower's electrical charge, the bee decides if it is worth visiting.

Ticks
READY TO SUCK YOUR BLOOD

Deer Tick

Like spiders and scorpions, ticks are arachnids. Ticks like to live in long grass and woods. While insects have three pairs of legs and one pair of antennae, ticks have four pairs of legs and no antennae. Ticks are a bit like vampires. After being born, they need blood to survive. So if you're out for a walk in the woods, try to stay on the trail and check your body when you get home. If you see a black dot on your skin, it might be a tick. Remove it very carefully!

NAME THAT BLOODSUCKER!

American Dog Tick

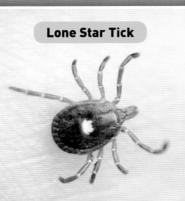

Lone Star Tick

HARD AND SOFT TICKS

Almost all ticks belong to one of two families. Ixodidae are hard ticks and are difficult to crush. Argasidae are soft ticks. Both hard and soft ticks get fat on blood. Hard ticks have their mouths at the front of their bodies. Soft ticks' mouths are on the underside of their bodies. All ticks have four stages to their lifecycle: egg, larva (newborn), nymph (child), and adult.

GETTING RID OF TICKS

To remove a tick from your skin or that of a friend or family member, grab a tick-remover (or a pair of tweezers or a tissue). Then grasp the tick as close to the skin as possible and pull it out. Do not use petroleum jelly, oil, or alcohol to kill the tick. The goal is to remove the creature's entire body.

HITCHHIKERS

Deer ticks like to lie in wait for a passing deer. Then they grab on for a long ride and a meal. The trouble is that deer ticks also like humans. Ticks will also grasp onto a passing person's clothes and crawl toward skin. Then they attach themselves and begin feeding. Deer ticks can cause Lyme disease, a treatable but serious illness.

GROWING UP

Cockroaches grow to maturity very quickly. A one-day-old roach (which is about the size of a speck of dust) can run as fast as its parents. Most cockroaches grow to adult size in 36 days.

Cockroaches

GET THE BUG SPRAY!

Many city dwellers know the creepy feeling of turning on a kitchen light to see a flurry of cockroaches scurrying across their countertops. Cockroaches are insects of the order Blattodea, which also includes termites. There are a walloping 4,600 species of these annoying critters and 30 of them are associated with human habitats. A cockroach can survive pretty much anywhere. Winter or summer, spring or fall, cockroaches appear to be here to stay.

DID YOU **KNOW?**

- Cockroaches have been around since long before the dinosaurs.
- A cockroach can live a month without food and almost two weeks without water.
- A cockroach can live for a week without its head!
- Cockroaches can hold their breath for up to 40 minutes.
- Cockroaches can run up to 3 mph (5 kph).

DRINKERS

It's hard to believe, but scientists have noticed that the American cockroach likes beer. Most likely, the bugs are attracted by the drink's hops and sugar.

THE WORLD'S LARGEST

Most people find large cockroaches especially hard to stomach. If you hate big bugs, stay away from South America. That's where one of the world's largest roaches lives. The giant cave cockroach can be up to 4 inches (10 centimeters) long with a 6-inch (15-centimeter) wingspan!

Dangerous Critters

PESTS THAT BITE, STING . . . OR WORSE!

These creepy crawlers are dangerous, damaging, and some are even deadly!

The bite of the female **black widow arachnid** can be very harmful to humans. Years ago, a bite by this scary spider was considered fatal. Today, with proper treatment, a bite is survivable, but not without some serious pain.

Bullet ants are found in Central and South America, from Nicaragua south to Paraguay. Their name comes from their sting, which feels like being shot. It is said that a run-in with one of these ants is 30 times as painful as a wasp sting. Locals also call these insects "24-hour ants" because of the full day of horrible pain they have after being stung.

Don't be fooled by the name **kissing bugs**. These blood-sucking insects can bite the faces of humans and other mammals. Then they hang on, transmitting a parasite called *Trypanosoma cruzi*. The kissing bug disease, or Chagas, kills 12,000 people a year.

Another species of ant to avoid is **fire ants**. These creatures bite attackers to get a grip, and then inject venom with a sting, causing great pain and in some extreme cases, death. Unfortunately, there are over 285 species of fire ants in the world.

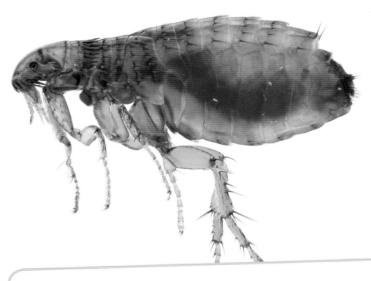

You might choose to avoid picking up a **house centipede** just because of its creepy appearance, and that would be a good decision. Even though it only has 15 pairs of legs and not 100, it has a pair of venomous claws. Their painful sting could give you a swelling that would last for days.

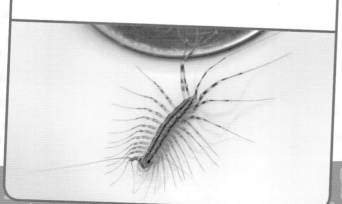

Fleas live on blood. A full-grown flea attaches itself to a bird or mammal, including humans, and starts sucking. The female flea consumes an amazing 15 times her own body weight in blood every single day! Pets with fleas may have bouts of intense, horrible itching and can even become infected with tapeworms if they eat fleas while grooming. Fleas can really leap, too. One of these little critters can jump 8 inches (20 centimeters) high—the equivalent of a person leaping over a skyscraper.

Worms

MORE THAN JUST **BAIT!**

FUN FACT!

Every earthworm is a hermaphrodite, which means it is both male and female.

They wiggle on the end of a fishing pole, slither on the sidewalk after a rainstorm, and dig their way through gardens. They're earthworms, and there are thousands of different species of them! Earthworms have no arms, legs, or eyes. They don't have lungs either, so they breathe through their skin. Their skin also produces a slick liquid that helps them slither underground through the dirt. Earthworms help plants grow by aerating the earth, and also through their poop, which contains more of the nutrient nitrogen than soil does.

EARTH-FRIENDLY CREATURES

Worms are actually excellent for the environment. On one acre of land, you might find more than a million earthworms!

• As an earthworm eats, it turns dead leaves, rotting fruit, and other organic waste into high-quality soil. Earthworms create compost that has more than 10 times the nutrients of ordinary soil.

• As food passes through an earthworm's digestive system, it is enriched with bacteria, which is good for the soil. A bunch of earthworms can reduce composting time from 240 to 30 days!

DID YOU KNOW?

If someone called you a slug, you'd probably be insulted. But slugs are actually interesting creatures.

• Slugs play an important part in the ecology of an area by eating rotten vegetation.

• Only 5% of the slug population is above ground at any time. The other 95% is deep in the dirt, laying eggs or eating.

• Like worms, slugs are both male and female.

• Slugs can live up to 6 years.

• Essentially, a slug is a snail without a shell.

• Slugs are mostly water, and will dry up if they're not kept moist enough.

• A slug smells with the tentacles on its head.

• Slugs can stretch out to 20 times their normal length!

Birds
NEST FRIENDS
FOREVER

What makes birds unique among other animals? It's the combination of powerful wings, hollow bones, and large, strong hearts that make most birds nearly perfect flying machines.

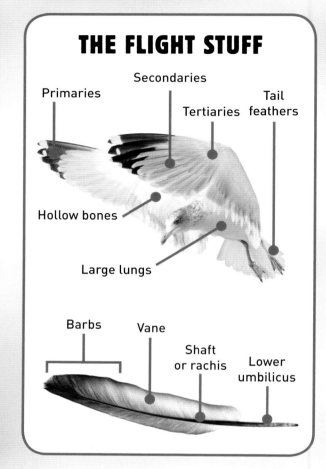

THE FLIGHT STUFF

Primaries

Secondaries

Tertiaries

Tail feathers

Hollow bones

Large lungs

Barbs

Vane

Shaft or rachis

Lower umbilicus

Sparrows

NAVIGATION EXPERTS

Birds have incredible navigational skills. Migratory birds are most impressive. They fly hundreds, even thousands, of miles each year back and forth to the same spots. Non-migratory birds are good navigators, too. They use their homing skills to find food and get back to their nests.

Golden Eagle

MALE OR FEMALE

How does a bird-watcher tell the difference between a male and a female bird? In many species, the male's colors are brighter. Females sport duller colors that make it easier for them to blend into their surroundings.

Northern Cardinals

CHIRPING

Birds are expert communicators and use elaborate songs and calls to talk to each other. For many species, all that chirping is part of courtship behavior. Mother birds chirp to their young. Each bird has a call unique to its species.

Red-backed Shrike

HOARDERS

Birds like blue jays, chickadees, and acorn woodpeckers hide food to eat at a later time. This behavior is more common with northern birds, who have to survive long, cold winters without a lot of food sources. The birds collect and hide hundreds—even thousands—of seeds, nuts, or acorns. Amazingly, the brains of some of these birds actually grow larger during the fall. This helps them remember where they hid the food.

Acorn Woodpecker

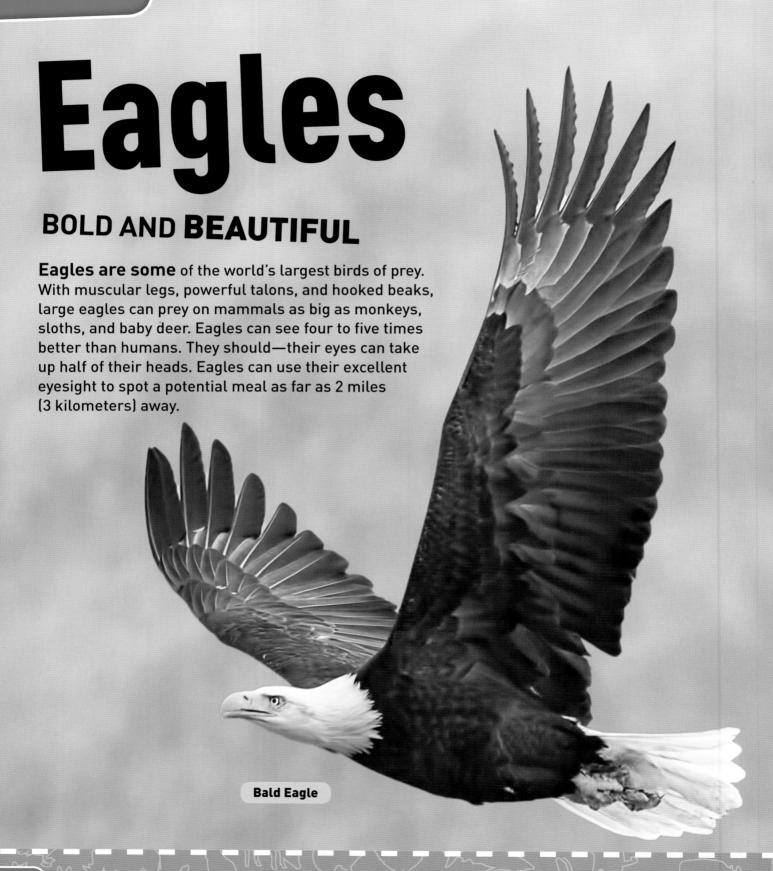

Eagles

BOLD AND **BEAUTIFUL**

Eagles are some of the world's largest birds of prey. With muscular legs, powerful talons, and hooked beaks, large eagles can prey on mammals as big as monkeys, sloths, and baby deer. Eagles can see four to five times better than humans. They should—their eyes can take up half of their heads. Eagles can use their excellent eyesight to spot a potential meal as far as 2 miles (3 kilometers) away.

Bald Eagle

DIFFERENT GROUPS, DIFFERENT MEALS

Eagles are classified into four groups–Sea eagles feed mostly on fish; booted eagles have a wide diet consisting of birds, small mammals, reptiles, rodents, and insects; snake eagles feast mostly on reptiles; giant forest eagles feed mainly on animals of the forest, including monkeys and sloths.

Sea Eagle

ALL SHAPES AND SIZES

Eagles vary greatly in size. Though most are large, one of the smallest species, the little eagle, is only 1.5 feet (0.5 meters) tall. The largest are over 3 feet (0.9 meters) tall with wingspans of up to 7 feet (2.1 meters).

Golden Eagle

BIRD EQUALITY

Eagles are loyal birds that mate for life. The "married" pair of birds uses the same nest year after year. The nest is built by both the male and female, working together. Eagles tend to lay between one and three eggs at a time.

THE BALD EAGLE

Known for its snowy-feathered head (not bald) and white tail, the bald eagle is the symbol of the United States. Sadly, the bird was nearly wiped out in North America in the early 1970s due to hunters and the poisonous pesticide DDT. But in 1972, DDT was restricted. Helped by reintroduction programs, the bald eagle has made a comeback. Today, bald eagles are thriving in Alaska and Canada.

OLD MAN OWL

Owls have been found in the fossil record up to 54 million years ago. These birds have been around for a long time.

DID YOU KNOW?

- Many owl species have asymmetrical ears, allowing them to pinpoint sounds in multiple directions.
- Owls can rotate their necks 270 degrees—that's almost all the way around!
- A group of owls is called a parliament. Baby owls are called owlets.
- Owls sometimes hunt other owls. Great horned owls are a top predator of the smaller barred owl.
- One of the tiniest owls in the world is the elf owl, measuring 6 in (15 cm) tall.
- Barn owls can eat over 1,000 mice, voles, and shrews a year.
- Owls eat their prey whole. Then they hack up the parts they can't digest, like bones, claws, and teeth, in tightly packed pellets.

OWL TALK

Owls say "whoo," but not every species hoots. In fact, owls can make a wide range of sounds, including screeches, whistles, barks, growls, rattles, and hisses.

Owls

WHOO GOES THERE?

Owls are the mysterious-looking birds that perch in trees and say "whoo!" These fierce predators are bad news for small mammals and rodents. As well as perching in trees, owls live in barns and cacti—and some even burrow in the ground. Owls have a unique upright posture and forward-facing eyes that give them what is called "binocular vision." Though they can focus in on objects very far away—usually prey—they don't see as well close-up. An owl has three eyelids: one for blinking, one for sleeping, and one for keeping the eye clean and healthy.

Eastern Screech Owl

Barred Owl

Some commonly found owls are:

Snowy Owl

Barn Owl

Western Screech Owl

Great Horned Owl

Falcons and hawks are birds of prey. Falcons kill with their beaks and hawks attack with the sharp talons on their feet. Adult falcons have thin wings that allow them to fly very fast and change direction on a dime. Hawks are mainly woodland birds with long tails and great eyesight. Goshawks are routinely trained by humans to hunt small game.

Hawks and Falcons

BIRDS OF **PREY**

PEREGRINE FALCONS

Peregrine falcons are among the world's most common birds of prey. Though they prefer wide-open spaces, these birds can be found in the desert, by the sea, and perched on the buildings of major cities. Falcons can catch smaller birds in midair with wild, thrilling dives called stoops. In cities, falcons feast on slow-flying pigeons. In the country, they love ducks and shorebirds. Maybe that's because a peregrine falcon can reach a diving speed of over 200 miles (322 kilometers) per hour.

NORTHERN GOSHAWKS

Northern goshawks are large birds, 20 to 23 inches (51 to 58 centimeters) tall with wingspans of 40 inches (1 meter). Goshawks like grouse, squirrels, rabbits, and small birds. Interestingly, a goshawk couple makes up to nine nests but only defends one of them each year. The empty nests are used by squirrels, owls, and other birds. Tough creatures, goshawks don't have many enemies to worry about and are only truly vulnerable during nesting time when hawks, owls, or tree-climbing bears might attack.

Peregrine Falcon

SOME ANIMALS ARE PICKY, PICKY EATERS

Vultures

When you picture a vulture, you probably think of a big, mangy bird that's cruising the skies waiting to feast on a dead zebra or wildebeest. Actually, there are 23 vulture species in the world, and they come in different shapes and sizes. At least one type of vulture can be found on every continent except Australia and Antarctica.

DID YOU KNOW?

- Vultures like to hang out in flocks called committees, volts, kettles, venues, or wakes, depending on what they're doing.

- A vulture's sense of smell is so powerful it can locate a dead animal from more than a mile (1.6 km) away!

- Vultures don't generally circle a sick animal waiting for it to die. They are more likely to swoop right in and start eating before another animal takes their meal.

- Yes, vultures mostly eat dead animals. But they are capable of going on the attack, especially if they are hungry.

- The Andean condor is the largest vulture in the world. It is found in South America, and it has a wingspan of about 11 ft (3 m)!

Since vultures have blunt talons, they often have to wait for other animals to rip open a dead body before they start the feast.

Vultures prefer fresh meat but usually consume rotted carcasses. Because of this, vultures help prevent the spread of disease from rotting animals.

Turkeys and Ducks
FOWL, FEATHERED FRIENDS

In America, turkeys are best known as a traditional Thanksgiving meal. But there are more interesting things about turkeys than their drumsticks. Turkeys are fowl, and ducks are waterfowl.

A BACHELOR PARTY

How do turkeys mate? Groups of related male turkeys like to band together to woo female turkeys (hens). Despite this teamwork, in the end, only one male gets the girl.

TURKEY FUN FACTS!

- A turkey is a distant relation of the *T. rex*.
- A turkey can sport multiple stylish beards.
- A turkey can fly at a speed of 50 mph (80 kph) in a short burst.
- Only male turkeys gobble. Each one has its own gobbling style to attract a mate. Female turkeys cluck and make small chirping noises.

DID YOU KNOW?

- The duck is in the Anatidae family of birds and is related to swans and geese.
- A male duck is called a drake, a female is a hen, and a baby is a duckling.
- Ducks are omnivores, feeding on plants as well as small fish, insects, and worms.
- The most common species of duck is the mallard or wild duck. It can live in the wild for 5 to 10 years.

QUACK QUACK WADDLE WADDLE

Ducks are normally found in marshes, oceans, rivers, ponds, and lakes. A duck has a special gland near its tail. The gland produces oil that spreads over its feathers, making them waterproof. A duck's feathers are also fluffy and soft, which helps keep it warm. Ducks tend to look for a mate in the winter, when the males will attract the females with their colorful feathers. The female lays between 5 and 12 eggs, which hatch within 28 days. Ducklings are able to fly within five to eight weeks.

Swans
AMAZING
AND
GRACEFUL

Swans are among the most beautiful creatures on the planet. Their pure white feathers and elegant, elongated necks make for a stunning picture on lakes and ponds. Swans eat by dipping their long necks into the water and foraging for plants. They nest near wetlands containing pondweed and line their nests with moss and grass.

Like geese and ducks, **swans** migrate thousands of miles a year to warmer climates for the winter. Swans can fly more than 3,500 miles (5,600 kilometers) or more on a round-trip between their summer and winter homes.

DID YOU KNOW?

- Swans mate for life.
- Black swans are native to Australia.
- A male swan is called a cob, a female swan is called a pen, and a baby is called a cygnet.
- The black-necked swan lives in South America.
- Swans can fly as fast as 60 mph (97 kph)!
- A group of wild swans is known as a herd. But a group in captivity is called a fleet.
- There are 6 different species of swan.
- The swan has over 25,000 feathers on its body.
- There are no swans living in Antarctica.

WATCH OUT!

Don't get too distracted by a swan's beauty. Swans can be nasty protectors of their turf, especially when they feel threatened. Moving quickly across the water, they can flap their enormous wings and hiss. Swans have even been known to attack people, so it's best to admire them from a safe distance.

Birds of Paradise
FABULOUS FLIERS

There is a family of birds called Paradisaeidae that lives in New Guinea and the surrounding islands (near Australia). With their colorful yellow, scarlet, and blue feathers, these birds are among the most beautiful on the planet. The males have long, elegant feathers called wires or streamers. Some species have exotic head plumes. Mother Nature delivered something truly gorgeous in these birds of paradise.

MATING RITUALS

Male birds of paradise are known for their wildly elaborate mating dances. They preen, they pose, and they show off their vibrant, colorful feathers. Their displays can go on for hours!

In 2012, *National Geographic* biologist-photographer Tim Laman and scientist Edwin Scholes successfully documented all 39 species of birds of paradise. It took them eight years of hard work. "This family of birds is a biological wonder of the world," said Scholes. They were even able to observe the **Arfak astrapia**, a long-tailed bird with green and black plumage that attracts a mate by hanging upside down from a branch.

FEAST YOUR EYES ON THESE FEATHERS!

Wilson's Bird of Paradise

Ptiloris

Bird-watching

I SPY... A YELLOW BELLIED SAPSUCKER!

Bird-watchers, or birders, are just ordinary folks who like to rise early in the morning, grab a pair of binoculars, and head into the woods to watch and listen for winged creatures.

NAME THAT TUNE

Part of bird-watching is learning to identify different bird calls. A recent poll picked the most interesting bird calls in the world. The top three were the common raven, the western meadowlark, and the Swainson's thrush.

Fire Island National Seashore, New York

READY TO **TRAVEL?**

Here are some great bird parks around the United States:

- Fire Island National Seashore, New York: over 300 species
- National Capital Parks, Washington, D.C.: over 300 species
- Cumberland Island National Seashore, Georgia: over 330 species
- Acadia National Park, Maine: over 360 species
- Lake Mead, Nevada and Arizona: over 240 species
- Everglades National Park, Florida: over 360 species
- Indiana Dunes National Lakeshore: over 270 species
- Carlsbad Caverns National Park, New Mexico: over 350 species
- Cape Hatteras National Seashore, North Carolina: 360 species
- Point Reyes National Seashore, California: almost 490 species

FUN **FACT!**

Scientists who study birds for a living are called ornithologists.

HOW TO BIRD-WATCH

Becoming a birder is actually quite easy. Here are four easy steps to get you started:

- Get some binoculars. This is essential for seeing birds in trees from afar.

- Buy a bird guide. Don't try to memorize all the birds, but browse through your guide. Learn about bird families (swallows, raptors, warblers, flycatchers, and so on). Then refer back to the book when you are out in the field to identify the birds you find.

- Take a walk! Check with your local Audubon chapter, nature center, or bird store. There might be bird walks posted.

- Use the Internet. This is another great way to investigate nearby places that attract a lot of birds and to help you identify what you've seen.

FIELD GUIDE

Birds

BY AIR

ON THE SHORE
AND OVER THE WAVES

Water Birds

Some birds like the forest. Some like meadows. Some are even city citizens. But some birds are beach lovers! Gulls, cranes, puffins, and the famous albatross are all birds of the sea.

Frigatebirds live near tropical waters. They can soar on the wind for weeks and spend most of their time flying over the ocean.

DID YOU **KNOW?**

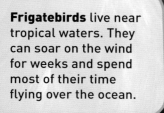

- There are 50 species of gulls throughout the world.
- Though they are called "seagulls," some species of this bird thrive far away from the ocean.
- Seagulls can drink either freshwater or saltwater.
- Seagulls are clever birds that play games with each other and are known to steal food from picnic areas.
- Seagulls mate for life.

140

MEET THE CRANES

Cranes are a family of large, long-legged, long-necked birds. They fly with their necks outstretched. Most cranes construct platform nests in shallow water and both parents help rear the young. What do cranes eat? Well, fish, of course!

In the 1800s and early 1900s, habitat loss and hunting brought the **whooping crane** to near extinction. By 1941, there were only 15 whooping cranes left in the world. These survivors all belonged to a single flock that migrated between Canada and Texas. Conservationists worked to protect the flock. Slowly but surely, their efforts paid off. By 1970, there were 57 whooping cranes. By 2005, there were 214. Even so, the younger whooping cranes needed to be taught how to migrate. To help them out, the International Whooping Crane Recovery Team used a light aircraft to guide the whooping cranes from western Florida to Wisconsin!

Albatross are giant seabirds with wingspans of up to 11 feet (3 meters). Using ocean winds, they can fly for hours with minimal effort, sometimes not even flapping their wings!

Atlantic puffins live at sea most of their lives. Though they fly through the air like most birds, they also "fly" across the water, using their wings as paddles and their webbed feet as rudders. Puffins are great at fishing. They can dive down to 200 feet (61 meters) and stay underwater for up to a minute, looking for a meal. In the spring and summer, thousands of puffins gather in colonies on the coast of the North Atlantic. Puffins mate for life and often return to the same burrow they used the year before.

Geese

LONG-DISTANCE TRAVELERS

The best-known geese in North America are from Canada. Canada geese are most easily identified by their long black necks and black heads, crowns, and bills. Their habitat includes ponds, lakes, rivers, grain fields, and freshwater and saltwater marshes, though some Canada geese have been settling in urban areas, putting them in closer contact with humans.

THE **FAMOUS V**

Canada geese migrate south each winter to find open water and grass. They are known for flying in a V formation. Scientists think the birds do this to conserve energy. When each bird flies slightly above the bird in front of him, it results in a reduction of wind resistance. Each bird takes a turn flying out front, and then falls to the back of the line when it gets tired. This way geese can log many miles before having to stop to rest. A V formation also helps the geese keep track of each other and helps with communication within the group.

WHAT'S IN A **NAME?**

The smallest Canada geese are called "cackling geese" because of their high-pitched squawks. The largest are called "honkers."

The male **Canada goose** is a fierce defender of his family and will charge an enemy. Some have been known to take on an elk!

DID YOU **KNOW?**

- A female is called a goose and a male is a gander. Offspring are goslings.
- The Canada goose has webbed feet for swimming.
- A group of many geese is called a flock, a chevron, or a string.

Colorful Birds

LET THE FASHION SHOW BEGIN!

Why do some birds have such fancy feathers? Scientists believe male birds sport many bright and beautiful colors to help them attract mates. The theory is that female birds think a male bird with lots of color is healthier and will take better care of their offspring. Experts also believe that birds are colorful because their ability to fly allows them to be less concerned about predators.

Peafowl

Mandarin Duck

Rainbow Lorikeet

Kingfisher

Lilac-breasted Roller

Scarlet Macaw

Toucan

Curl-crested Aracari

City Birds

LIFE ON THE LEDGE

CITY **STRESSES**

The busy pace of city life can be stressful for humans—but what about birds? A recent study has suggested that city life may make birds age more quickly! Even so, most cities' pigeon populations don't seem to be in a hurry to move back to the country. In New York City, it is believed there is at least one pigeon per person—that's 8.5 million birds!

PIGEONS IN AMERICA

The three most common city birds are the starling, sparrow, and pigeon. That's because they are very adaptable species, ready to eat almost anything and nest anywhere. City birds eat nuts, insects, worms, and slugs. Not dependent on trees or grass, these birds have no trouble living in the world of cement.

Pigeons first came to North America in the 1600s with French settlers, who used them for meat. Before long, the pigeons escaped. With natural predators like hawks and falcons scarce, and food readily available, the birds thrived. Today, an average city pigeon's life span is three to five years.

FEED THE BIRDS?

"Rats with wings!" That's what some city dwellers call their local birds. In a way, it's hard to blame them. City birds pick at garbage, aren't particularly colorful or interesting-looking, and poop on everything. But they have their fans. Courtney Humphries, author of *Superdove: How the Pigeon Took Manhattan . . . And the World*, has this to say about humans who feed the birds: "If nobody fed pigeons, I think things would look a lot different. A lot of the problem with pigeons comes from people."

Small Birds

TINY FLUTTERINGS

Get out your magnifying glass and take a peek at some of nature's smallest fliers.

Verdin
Native to North America

Red-cheeked Cordon-bleu
Native to Africa

American Goldfinch
Native to North America

Goldcrest
Native to Europe

Pardalote
Native to Australia

Tropical Parula
Native to South and
Central America

Bananaquit
Native to South and
Central America and
the Caribbean

THE SMALLEST OF THEM ALL

The bee hummingbird is about 3 inches (8 centimeters) long and weighs 0.1 ounce (3 grams), less than a sheet of paper! Their hearts can beat over 1,000 times in a minute! (Yours probably beats less than 100 times per minute when you're resting.) Native to Cuba, these little birds feed on flower nectar and tiny insects.

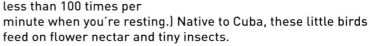

Bats

UPSIDE DOWN AND IN THE AIR

The only mammal that can fly, with three vampire species, bats are also the only mammals known to feed on blood. Though bats are often a part of scary bedtime stories, they are actually helpful to humans. Bats do a great public service by eating tons of insects. Some bat species also transfer pollen from one tree or plant to another, and they help with seed dispersal. Many farmers depend on bats to control the pests that can destroy their crops. Bats make up an astonishing one-fifth of the mammal population in the world, and there are over 1,000 different species of bats in the world. Some bats live together in groups called colonies in trees, barns, and caves—anywhere that will provide shelter for their young. Bats are nocturnal, meaning they sleep all day long and forage for food at night.

DID YOU KNOW?

- Bats can live up to 30 years and fly at speeds of 60 mph (97 kph).
- Bats find their food in complete darkness by emitting high-pitched sounds and listening to the echoes.
- Brown bats can eat up to 1,200 mosquitoes an hour.
- Some bats hibernate through winter and can survive even after becoming encased in ice.
- Bat droppings, called guano, are one of the richest fertilizers in the world.

YUMMY!

Seventy percent of bats eat insects, but some bats prefer less buggy meals. There are fruit-eating bats, nectar-eating bats, meat-eating bats, and fish-eating bats. Most famously, there are vampire bats in South America who feed on blood.

ALL SHAPES AND SIZES

Bumblebee Bat

Flying Fox Bat

The largest bat is the flying fox from the islands of the South Pacific. This impressive creature has a wingspan of up to 6 feet (2 meters)! The world's smallest bat is the bumblebee bat of Thailand. It's no more than an 1.5 inches (4 centimeters) long and weighs less than a dime.

Bees

WHAT'S THE BUZZ?

Bees live together in family units called colonies. The queen bee is the head of the family—it's her job to lay all the eggs. Worker bees are also female. They keep the hive, the structure the bees live in, clean. They also fly from flower to flower, collecting pollen and nectar to feed the colony. Pollen from one flower sticks to the hairs on a bee's body and rubs off on another flower, helping the process of pollination. That makes more flowers grow! Male bees are drones. Their only job is to mate with the queen.

Honeybee

DID YOU KNOW?

- There are 20,000 species of bees.
- Bees feed on nectar and pollen, dipping their long tongues to drink up nectar.
- It takes about 12 worker bees three weeks to make one teaspoon of honey.
- Bees make honey to feed their young and so they have food during the winter.
- Beekeepers use smoke to calm bees when collecting honey.

Honeybee

Paper Wasp

BEE OR WASP?

HONEYBEES	PAPER WASPS
• Live in wax hives	• Live in papery nests
• Have fatter hairy bodies and legs	• Have thinner smooth bodies and legs
• Feed on pollen and nectar	• Feed on other insects and spiders
• Most species are not aggressive	• Most species are aggressive

A DEATHLY STING

Sure, a bee sting can hurt a person—but it can kill the bee! That's because some bees' stingers have barbs and hooks on them. When this type of bee stings, the barbs and hooks catch onto the skin. When the bee flies away, the stinger and part of the bee's abdomen is ripped away. Ouch!

SUPER SENSES

Bees see all colors except red. They can even see some colors that are invisible to humans. Their extraordinary sense of sight, along with their sense of smell, helps a bee find flowers to collect nectar and pollen.

Butterflies

NATURE'S FLOATING FASHION SHOW

From the tiny western pygmy blue, with a 0.5-inch (1.2-centimeter) wingspan, to the Queen Alexandra's birdwing, which spreads out to nearly 1 foot (0.3 meters), butterflies come in many sizes and colors. They all go through the same four life phases, though.

Phase 1: Egg
Butterflies lay eggs on plant leaves. Some butterfly eggs are round, others oval, some are even ribbed.

Phase 2: Larva
When the egg hatches, a larva, or caterpillar, is born. At this stage, its main goal is to eat and grow.

Phase 3: Pupa or Chrysalis
As soon as the caterpillar has reached maturity, it attaches to a twig or leaf. It then sheds its outside layer of skin, revealing a hard skin underneath known as the pupa or chrysalis. Inside the pupa, one of the miracles of nature occurs: The caterpillar undergoes a transformation called metamorphosis and turns slowly into a butterfly.

Phase 4: Butterfly
Once the butterfly is fully formed, it emerges from the pupa. Blood pumps into its wings to get them working. Within hours, it is ready to fly!

THE MIGRATING BUTTERFLY

Monarch butterflies really know how to fly. Every year, monarch butterflies travel up to 1,500 miles (2,400 kilometers) to a cool habitat for the winter. In the spring, they fly north to find milkweed, then lay eggs. Once the caterpillars hatch, they wait to grow into fully formed butterflies before flying all the way back to the place where their "mother" first lived.

DID YOU KNOW?

- There are about 20,000 different species of butterflies.
- Butterflies attach their eggs to leaves with a special natural glue.
- Most caterpillars are herbivores, but some are predatory carnivores, and a few may even resort to cannibalism if they can't find enough food.
- Butterflies live as mature adults for anywhere from a week to a year, depending upon the species.
- Most butterflies feed on nectar from flowers.
- Butterflies have taste receptors on their feet!

Blue Morpho Butterfly

THAT'S EPIC!

Cicadas have fascinated many people and cultures. In ancient Greece and China, the cicada was seen as a powerful symbol of rebirth and immortality.

GOTTA LOVE THAT TREE SAP!

Cicadas reproduce when females lay 200 to 600 eggs in tiny holes made in branches and twigs. When the baby cicadas, called nymphs, hatch, they immediately burrow underground and attach to tree roots. The nymphs stay put, sucking tree sap for most of their lives. Finally, guided by instinct, the cicada climbs the trunk of a tree and sheds its skin, becoming an adult.

Cicadas

THE **TREE** CRICKETS

Cicadas are oval-shaped, winged insects that buzz and click. There are over 3,000 species of cicadas. Their bodies can be black, brown, or green, and they can have red, white, or blue eyes. When held up to the light, a cicada's wings look transparent.

SING IT OUT!

Cicadas are known as the world's noisiest insect. Their shrill buzzing sound is created by small drum-like plates. The cicada vibrates its abdomen, where the plates can be found. Why all that noise anyway? The male cicada makes a racket to attract the interest of a female. In other words, it is a mating call. A group of cicadas can be heard up to one mile (1.6 kilometers) away!

COME OUT TO **PLAY!**

While most cicadas come out every summer, some emerge only now and then. That's because there are two groups of cicadas: annual cicadas and periodical cicadas. Both types live underground for several years. Annual cicadas mature and emerge at different times, so some appear every year. Periodical cicadas mature all at the same time, so they come out to breed every 13 or 17 years. To add to the confusion, these bugs are sometimes called "17-year locusts," even though cicadas and locusts are NOT the same thing. (Locusts are a species of grasshopper.) Once cicadas finally make an appearance, their time on Earth is relatively short. Seventeen-year cicadas live for about four or five weeks above ground, and then die.

Praying Mantis

THE GREEN MONSTER

Praying mantises are a big group of insects—there are more than 2,400 species! Since they are carnivores, farmers once thought they would be great for getting rid of other insects that eat crops. However, they didn't count on them eating *every* insect, including the bees needed to spread pollen so that the crops would grow. Oops!

FUN FACT!

A praying mantis can turn its head 180 degrees, making it easy for the mantis to look over its shoulder.

KILLER CAMOUFLAGE

Different mantis species blend in so closely with leaves and flowers that it was believed they were masters of camouflage. It turns out, it's not camouflage at all. Scientists discovered that, while the orchid mantis does mimic the look of the orchid, it doesn't actually hide in that flower. Insects are even more attracted to the orchid mantis than the flower it is named after. That's called "aggressive mimicry," and it is used to lure in prey.

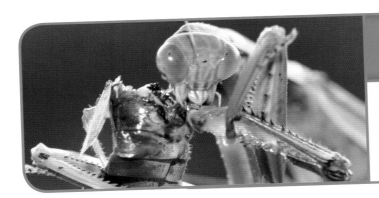

OUCH!

During mating, the female mantis will sometimes bite off her male partner's head!

LIFE CYCLE OF A PRAYING MANTIS

In late autumn, the female praying mantis will lay 100 to 400 eggs. The eggs are laid in a case called the ootheca.

Young praying mantises are born in the spring. They are called nymphs.

An adult praying mantis lives for six months.

Annoying Insects

Some insects are beautiful, some are helpful, but others are just flat out harmful and annoying!

TINY TERRORS

NOT IN MY HOUSE!

Termites are small, pale insects that live in large colonies. If you see a swarm of them fly by, it means your house is infested—and that's a big problem. They are known for their hugely destructive effect. Known as the "silent destroyers" because of their ability to gnaw through wood, termite colonies eat nonstop! The 2,000 different species of this hungry bug cause an estimated $5 billion in property damage each year in the United States.

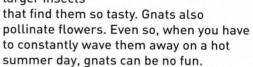

Gnats are very tiny insects that like to swarm—often around a person's face. Has a gnat ever flown in your eye? Maybe you've swallowed one by accident? Annoying, right? They're not so annoying to the birds, bats, and larger insects that find them so tasty. Gnats also pollinate flowers. Even so, when you have to constantly wave them away on a hot summer day, gnats can be no fun.

Japanese giant hornets live in rural parts of Japan. Generally, they like to be left alone. That's a good thing because this dangerous insect can kill an allergic human with a single sting.

Mosquitoes might well be the most dangerous insect on Earth. This annoying bug causes a half-million deaths a year by transmitting the disease malaria. It has been estimated that a child dies due to malaria every two minutes! Along with this dreaded disease (mostly found in Africa), mosquitoes can also spread dengue fever, yellow fever, encephalitis, and West Nile virus. Mosquito nets are an effective and inexpensive way to prevent these diseases.

Watch out for **tsetse flies** if you travel to the sub-Saharan region of Africa. They are blood-sucking flies in the housefly family. They carry parasites called trypanosomes, which cause sleeping sickness in humans. Without proper treatment, this disease can be deadly.

**Glasswing
Butterfly**

LIGHT **SHOW**

Along Thailand's Mae Klong River, fireflies put on a nightly show: They blink in absolute, perfect unison! No one knows exactly why, except that this action is part of their mating ritual. So, how do they do it? First, a small group starts to blink together. Next, another group joins in, and then another and another, until all the fireflies on the river are blinking as one. And the fireflies of Thailand aren't the only ones that blink in unison. This behavior has been observed in other groups of lightning bugs around the world.

Colorful Insects

FLUTTERING, FLOATING, AND FESTIVE

Ladybug

You might not think most insects are particularly attractive creatures. They're usually brown or green, and some can look downright scary. But there are some insects that defy the odds. They make the leap from ordinary or frightening to absolutely beautiful!

Peacock Butterfly

Dragonfly

Blue Pansy

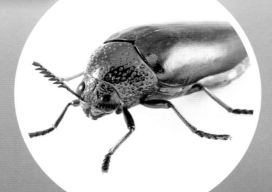

Jewel Beetle

Noisy Insects

KEEP IT **DOWN!**

Some insects can be noisy neighbors. Long-horned beetles squeak, hiss, or make a strumming sound when picked up. Crickets, grasshoppers, and katydids sing to attract mates. Bees and mosquitoes buzz. Aquatic insects make noise, too—you just have to be underwater to hear them.

LOOK CLOSELY, GRASSHOPPER

- Grasshoppers make a singing sound by rubbing their hind legs against their wings.

- A grasshopper is capable of eating half its body weight in plants each day.

- There are 11,000 species of grasshoppers in the world. They like to live in grassy fields, meadows, and forests.

- The average grasshopper is 2 in (5 cm) long, though some can grow to be as long as 5 in (13 cm).

- Grasshoppers are often colored to blend in with their environments—green for grassy fields, and brown for dirt and desert areas.

- Grasshoppers can jump more than 3 ft (0.9 m). That's even more impressive when you look at it this way: If a human could jump like a grasshopper, he or she could leap the length of a football field in a single bound!

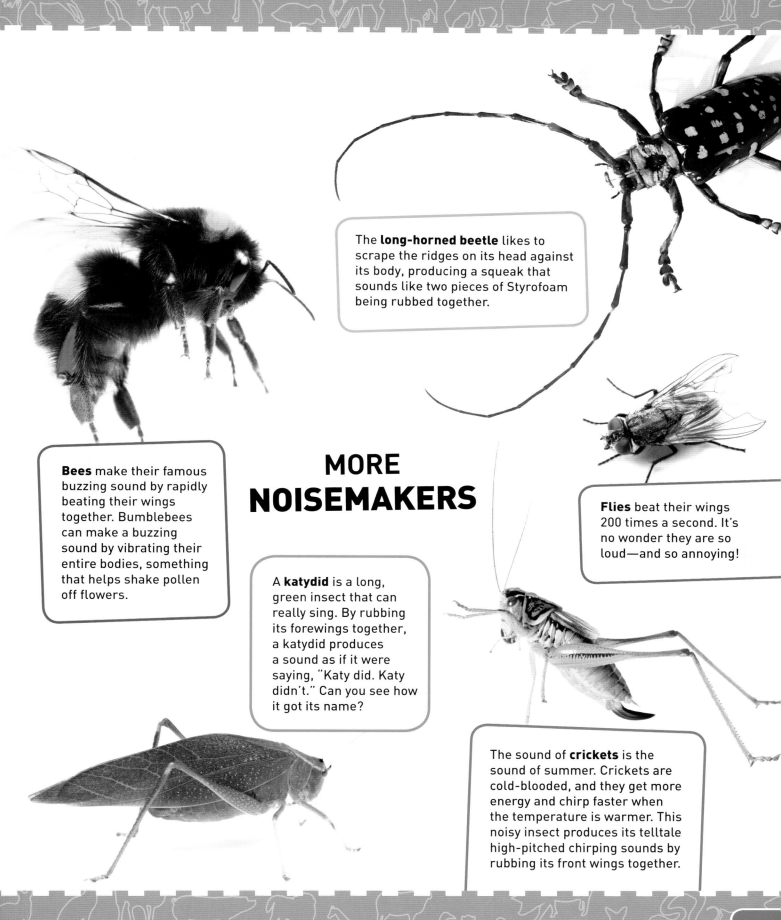

The **long-horned beetle** likes to scrape the ridges on its head against its body, producing a squeak that sounds like two pieces of Styrofoam being rubbed together.

MORE
NOISEMAKERS

Bees make their famous buzzing sound by rapidly beating their wings together. Bumblebees can make a buzzing sound by vibrating their entire bodies, something that helps shake pollen off flowers.

A **katydid** is a long, green insect that can really sing. By rubbing its forewings together, a katydid produces a sound as if it were saying, "Katy did. Katy didn't." Can you see how it got its name?

Flies beat their wings 200 times a second. It's no wonder they are so loud—and so annoying!

The sound of **crickets** is the sound of summer. Crickets are cold-blooded, and they get more energy and chirp faster when the temperature is warmer. This noisy insect produces its telltale high-pitched chirping sounds by rubbing its front wings together.

Dolphins

INTELLIGENT SWIMMERS

Bottlenose Dolphin

Dolphins are aquatic mammals. Even though they live in the water, they breathe air, nurse their babies with milk, are warm-blooded, and have hair at some point in their lives—just like all mammals. Most dolphins live in saltwater, but some species can thrive in freshwater, like a river. Dolphins travel in groups called pods. Pods are usually made up of 2 to 40 dolphins, but in areas where there are a lot of food sources, many pods can merge together to form a superpod of thousands of dolphins!

DID YOU KNOW?

- Dolphins are very intelligent animals.
- Dolphins are meat eaters.
- Bottlenose dolphins are the most common and well-known type of dolphin.
- Dolphins breathe out of a blowhole on the top of their heads.
- The killer whale, also known as the orca, is actually a type of dolphin.

Orca

SAD, BUT TRUE

Every year, many dolphins die when they are accidentally caught in giant fishing nets. Some dolphin species even face the threat of extinction. The Yangtze River dolphin was thought to be extinct, but Chinese conservationists believe they may have spotted one in 2016.

THAT MAKES SENSE

Dolphins have good eyesight, sharper hearing than humans, and a highly developed sense of touch. They can taste only salty flavors, though, and it is believed that they can't smell at all.

THE GREAT COMMUNICATORS

Dolphins communicate by clicking and whistling. These sound waves travel through the water and blend together with great complexity. Dolphins can express information and feelings about everything from food locations to danger. They can hear frequencies that are 10 times higher than humans can hear.

OCEAN SINGERS

Do humpback whales really sing? They do, especially when they are migrating or mating. Not only that, but the humpback tends to repeat the same chorus for up to 30 minutes at a time. The sounds can travel up to 100 miles (161 kilometers)!

A BIG APPETITE

Since whales are so large, it's no surprise that they need a lot of food. On average, a whale will eat four percent of its body weight per day—if there is enough food around. Baleen whales can eat as much as four tons (3.6 metric tons) of tiny krill a day. Whales are able to go a long time without food because of their blubber—an extra layer of fat that they build up when food is plentiful.

The largest known mammal that has ever lived, the **blue whale** is 100 feet (30 meters) long and weighs 150 tons (136,080 kilograms). It is also the largest living animal. How much food does such an enormous creature need to survive? A blue whale can hold up to 2,200 pounds (998 kilograms) of food in its stomach!

Whales
WORLD'S BIGGEST MAMMALS

Though they live in water, whales are mammals that feed milk to their babies. Since they are not fish, they don't have gills to breathe underwater. Instead, they breathe through a blowhole on the top of their heads. Whales migrate, or travel, farther than any other mammal. Scientists tracked a gray whale that swam 6,800 miles (10,880 kilometers) in 69 days, from her feeding grounds near Russia, across the Pacific Ocean, and down to Baja California, Mexico. Why travel all that way? Whales live in cold water where there is lots of krill, little fish, and other good things to eat. When it gets even colder and those food sources become scarce, they migrate to warm waters to have babies.

Orca

LIFE'S A BREACH

No one knows exactly why whales breach, or leap out of the water. Some scientists believe they are showing off to find a partner. They could also be looking out for predators or alerting other whales to nearby food. Breaching can help a whale to get water out of its lungs, too. Or they may just be playing and having fun—breaching does create an awesome splash!

Seals and Sea Lions

FLIPPING FOR FLIPPERS

Harbor Seal

Seals and sea lions are semiaquatic mammals that belong to a group called pinnipeds, which means "fin-footed." To tell the difference between seals and sea lions, check out their ears. True seals have no visible ears. Also, the flippers of seals point backward. Seals move on land with an up-and-down rocking motion. Sea lions can rotate their hind feet and move much faster on land.

SIZING THEM UP

There are 18 species of true seals. The largest is the southern elephant seal, a creature that can tip the scale at 8,800 pounds (3,992 kilograms) and stretch out to 20 feet (6 meters)! The smallest specimen is the ringed seal. It's 5 feet (1.5 meters) long and weighs only 150 pounds (68 kilograms).

Elephant Seals

BRRR . . . IT'S COLD!

True seals like areas where it's cold. Most live in the Arctic or off the coasts of Antarctica. They eat fish, eel, squid, octopus, and lobster.

Weddell Seal

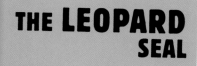

THE LEOPARD SEAL

One of the largest seals in the world is Antarctica's leopard seal. This extra-large pinniped can grow up to 10 feet (3 meters) long and weigh up to 1,300 pounds (590 kilograms). Though leopard seals can be friendly, they are aggressive enough to eat smaller seals for breakfast. They also have been known to attack people.

DID YOU KNOW?

- Sea lions are endangered due to overhunting.
- A male sea lion is called a bull, a female is called a cow, and a baby is a pup.
- A male sea lion can weigh up to 2,500 lbs (1,134 kg) and be 11 ft (3 m) long. It can eat up to 125 lbs (57 kg) of food a day.
- A female sea lion can weigh up to 770 lbs (349 kg) and be 9.5 ft (3 m) long. It can eat up to 40 lbs (18 kg) of food a day.
- A baby sea lion is 15 to 50 lbs (7 to 23 kg) at birth.
- Sea lions can walk on all four flippers.
- A sea lion can live up to 35 years in captivity and up to 20 years in the wild.
- The sea lion's two most dangerous predators are the shark and the killer whale.

Steller Sea Lion

SHOWSTOPPERS

There are six living species of sea lions (the Japanese sea lion became extinct in the 20th century). The most recognizable is the California sea lion—they're the stars of often-misnamed "seal" shows. California sea lions are intelligent and social animals, which makes them easy to train. In the wild, they are speed swimmers, reaching speeds of up to 25 miles (40 kilometers) per hour in the water—faster than any other seal or sea lion.

California Sea Lion

Walrus GENTLE CREATURE

Walruses are among the largest pinnipeds in the world. Known for their two very large tusks and distinguished mustaches, walruses are enormous, weighing between 1,300 and 3,300 pounds (590 and 1,497 kilograms). They are gentle giants, though, and not aggressive. The typical walrus is content to sit on an ice bank and relax. Their large, flabby bodies are covered in brown or pink skin. The skin is covered in short fur.

TUSK, TUSK

Walruses' tusks are their own personal tools. Using their tusks, they can pull themselves out of the water onto an ice shelf or break breathing holes into the ice from down below. Both male and female walrus tusks keep growing throughout a walrus's life. The tusks are actually very large canine teeth that grow to be 3 feet (1 meter) long.

LOVE THAT COLD WEATHER

A walrus's body is covered with blubber to keep it warm. More impressively, they are able to slow down their heartbeats to help them withstand the freezing-cold water. The slow heartbeat also allows them to stay underwater for as long as 10 minutes.

DID YOU KNOW?

- It takes about 15 months for a baby walrus to be born.
- A walrus's long, highly sensitive whiskers, called vibrissae, help them to find food on the ocean floor.
- Walruses can stay awake for more than three days straight, swimming nearly the whole time.
- They make up for lost sleep by dozing deeply for up to 19 hours—anywhere! They can sleep standing, leaning, floating on water, and even hanging onto an ice floe with their tusks.

Fish

JUST KEEP
SWIMMING

Fish are a class of aquatic vertebrates that lives in water. They breathe by taking in oxygen through gills. Fish also have fins, and most have skeletons made of bone—except sharks and rays, whose skeletons are made of cartilage. Scientists say there are more than 30,000 species of fish in the world. At 40 feet (12 meters) long, the largest fish is the whale shark. The smallest, at 0.33 inches (0.8 centimeters), is *Paedocypris progenetica.*

DID YOU **KNOW?**

- Fish had been swimming around the planet for about 250 million years before mammals evolved.

- Fish species outnumber the combined total of amphibian, bird, mammal, and reptile species.

- The fastest fish on Earth—the sailfish, swordfish, and marlin—can reach speeds of up to 70 mph (113 kph).

- The rougheye rockfish can live more than 200 years, and the Greenland shark lives over 270!

- Hagfish, one of the most primitive fish, are also known as slime eels. That's because they produce a truly gross amount of mucus when disturbed. In minutes, just one hagfish can fill a 2-galllon (8-liter) bucket with slime.

Marlin

Body by Design

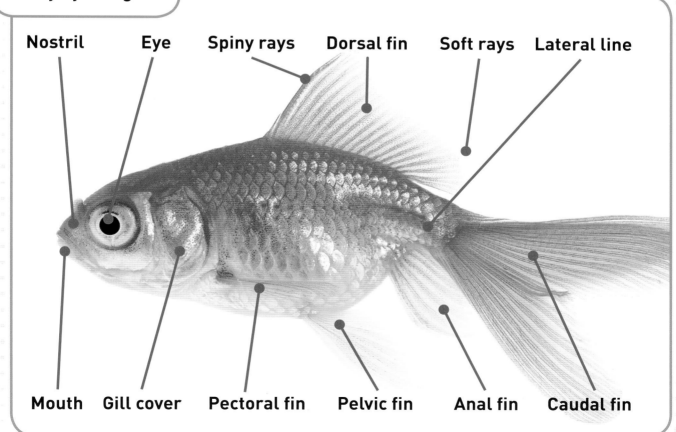

Nostril   Eye   Spiny rays   Dorsal fin   Soft rays   Lateral line

Mouth   Gill cover   Pectoral fin   Pelvic fin   Anal fin   Caudal fin

Sharks

SEA PREDATORS

Though many of the 500 or so shark species are really large, some are very small. The dwarf lantern shark is only 6 inches (15 centimeters) long! On the other end of the shark growth chart is the whale shark. At 40 feet (12 meters), it is enormous—and terrifying-looking. But you don't have to worry about them: They feed only on plankton. Just make sure you don't swim in front of one—you could be sucked into its enormous mouth. While most sharks live in the ocean, some, such as the bull shark, live in rivers.

Bull Shark

ENDLESS TEETH

Sharks have between five and seven rows of teeth in their mouths, arranged in layers. Amazingly, if a tooth breaks off, another one grows in its place within a day. In fact, sharks can lose and then grow up to 20,000 teeth in their lives. After a shark dies, its teeth will take about 10,000 years to fossilize.

Whale Shark

DID YOU **KNOW?**

- Sharks have been swimming Earth's oceans for about 400 million years. They were on the planet before dinosaurs!

- Despite their reputation as killers of people, 97% of shark species pose no real threat to us.

- The prehistoric shark megalodon probably grew to 60 ft (18 m).

- Sharks are at the top of the underwater food chain and have no serious animal predators. Humans, however, kill upward of 100 million sharks a year.

PICKY EATERS? **NOT!**

Sharks are carnivores that eat other fish—lots of them. But on the way to finding a proper meal, they will ingest pretty much anything. Through the years, some strange things have been found in sharks' stomachs, including tires, bike parts, license plates, cannonballs, and even bottles of wine!

Hammerhead Shark

Great White Shark

GIANT FISH WITH A MIGHTY BITE

DID YOU KNOW?

- Unlike most sharks, great white sharks are partly warm-blooded. They can regulate their own body temperature, so they are comfortable in both cold and warm ocean water.
- Great white sharks are the largest predatory fish on the planet.
- The "white" part of the shark's name refers to its white underbelly.
- A great white shark can eat 11 tons (9,979 kg) of food a year.

It's easy to see how the great white shark got its name. It's huge! At birth, a great white is already 5 feet (1.5 meters) long. At maturity, it may reach 15 to 20 feet (five to six meters). Great whites have massive jaws with a set of 300 sharp teeth. When they are young, great white sharks feed on small prey, such as fish and rays. When they're older, they eat sea lions, seals, and small whales. Great whites like to take their prey by surprise, positioning themselves underneath their victim before exploding upward with their mouths open wide. Often, they burst out of the water in a leap—called a breach—with their meal already in their mouths. They rip the flesh off their catch, piece by piece, and swallow the pieces whole.

IT'S ALL IN THE NOSE

Seals have to keep their distance from the great white shark. Sharks can smell a colony of seals up to 2 miles (3 kilometers) away!

WATCH OUT FOR MOM!

When a great white shark gives birth, her pups are immediately on their own. Not only that, they have to swim away fast, or the mother shark might try to eat them!

YUCK!

About 5 to 10 instances of great white sharks attacking people are reported each year. Unfortunately, sharks sometimes mistake us for delicious sea lions or seals. Fortunately, humans don't taste very good to sharks. If a great white takes a big bite out of an unlucky surfer or swimmer, the shark typically spits it out.

Weird Water Dwellers

GIANT **SQUID!**
KILLER **PIRANHA!**
DEADLY **OCTOPUS!**

THE **SCARY** EIGHT

There may be as many as eight species that fall into the group of giant squid. Usually, the females are a good 10 feet (3 meters) longer than the males. The squid's unique body allows it to move like lightning in the water, which makes escape very difficult for its prey.

The giant squid is one of the largest invertebrates, or animals without a backbone, on Earth. The largest giant squid ever found measured a whopping 43 feet (13 meters) and weighed nearly a ton (0.9 metric tons)! Still, since these massive, mysterious creatures are so rare and live so deep in the ocean, most of what we've learned about them comes from remains that have washed up on beaches. Like all squid species, giant squid have eight arms and two long tentacles. They use their tentacles to bring food to their beak-like mouth. Giant squid have eyes as large as basketballs—the largest eyes of any creature on the planet. Their diet consists of fish, shrimp, and other squid.

Piranhas live in lakes and rivers in South America. "Piranha" means "tooth fish" in the language of the Tupi people of Brazil, and these swimmers are famous for their razor-sharp, triangular teeth. The red piranha is the largest of the 20 piranha species in the Amazon and can grow to 14 inches (36 centimeters). Piranha are more likely to eat other fish and shrimp than to nibble on a human. Still, occasional attacks on human swimmers have been reported. Whatever they are eating, piranhas are incredibly aggressive. When going in for a kill, this fish has been known to bark!

Bigfin Reef Squid

The **blue-ringed octopus** of Australia and Japan is regarded as one of the most venomous animals in the world. Though they look cute, these deadly creatures live in shallow tidal pools and will attack waders who accidentally step their way, releasing a deadly venom that can kill in minutes. There is no anti-venom that will counteract the venom of the blue-ringed octopus. Once bitten, there is little hope.

Lobsters

TWO "CLAWS"
FOR COMFORT

Lobsters are 10-legged crustaceans, a type of invertebrate with a hard exoskeleton. They are closely related to shrimp and crabs. Though they can be found all over the world, lobsters thrive in the cold seas of the northern Atlantic. Lobsters don't see very well, but they make up for their poor eyesight with a highly developed sense of taste and smell. They feed mostly on fish and mollusks. Unfortunately for lobsters, people love to eat them. As a result, trapping lobster has turned into a multibillion-dollar-a-year industry.

LOBSTER BABIES

A lobster mother carries her eggs for up to a year inside her body. Then, she spends another 9 to 12 months carrying them under her tail!

THE POOR MAN'S CHICKEN

Lobster was so plentiful during colonial times in the U.S., it was known as "the poor man's chicken." Back then, lobster was fed to pigs and goats! Wealthy people wouldn't eat it, thinking it was only good for the poor. Today, lobster is a pricey delicacy.

DID YOU KNOW?

- Lobsters turn red when cooked. In nature, they can be green, yellow, or bright blue.
- Lobsters are crustaceans, which are also arthropods—like insects. Because of this, lobsters are nicknamed "bugs."
- Lobsters are usually caught in an underwater trap called a lobster pot, which is baited with fish.
- Lobsters can grow to 3.5 ft (1.1 m) and weigh up to 40 lbs (18 kg). They can live over 50 years.
- There are about 6,000 licensed lobstermen in the state of Maine.

WALK LIKE A CRAB

Some crabs have a distinct sideways walk. They also swim sideways. But there are others that can walk and swim forward and backward.

Ghost Crab

OLD MAN CRAB

Crabs are an ancient species, first appearing on Earth during the Jurassic Period, about 200 million years ago. Crabs come in all sizes. The smallest species, the pea crab, is barely a half inch (1.2 centimeters) long. The largest, the Japanese spider crab, has a claw-to-claw leg span of 12 feet (4 meters).

Japanese Spider Crab

DID YOU KNOW?

- Crabs communicate with each other by waving their pincers.
- Crabs are omnivores—they eat meat and plants.
- Some species of crab can shed a limb and naturally grow it back within a year.

Kelp Crab

FUN FACT!

Because they have 10 legs, crabs are known as decapods.

Crabs

THEY DO IT IN A PINCH

The crab is another member of the crustacean family. There are more than 4,500 species of crab in the world, found in salty, fresh, or brackish (salty and fresh) waters. Though most species of crab live in the water, some live on land, making homes in sandy areas with stones and rocks. Like fish, most crabs breathe with the help of gills, so they need to keep water close at all times.

River Crab

Jellyfish

DON'T PASS
THE PEANUT BUTTER!

Even though the word "fish" is in their name, jellyfish aren't really fish at all. Rather, they are invertebrates that live in fresh or ocean water. Some jellyfish are larger than a human, and others are smaller than a penny. They come in many colors, from clear to pink, yellow, blue, and purple. Made up of water and protein, jellyfish move by squirting water from their mouths. They hunt by stinging prey with their tentacles. Though it's hard to see, inside a jellyfish's bell-shaped body is its mouth. Amazingly, this strange invertebrate eats and releases waste from this same opening.

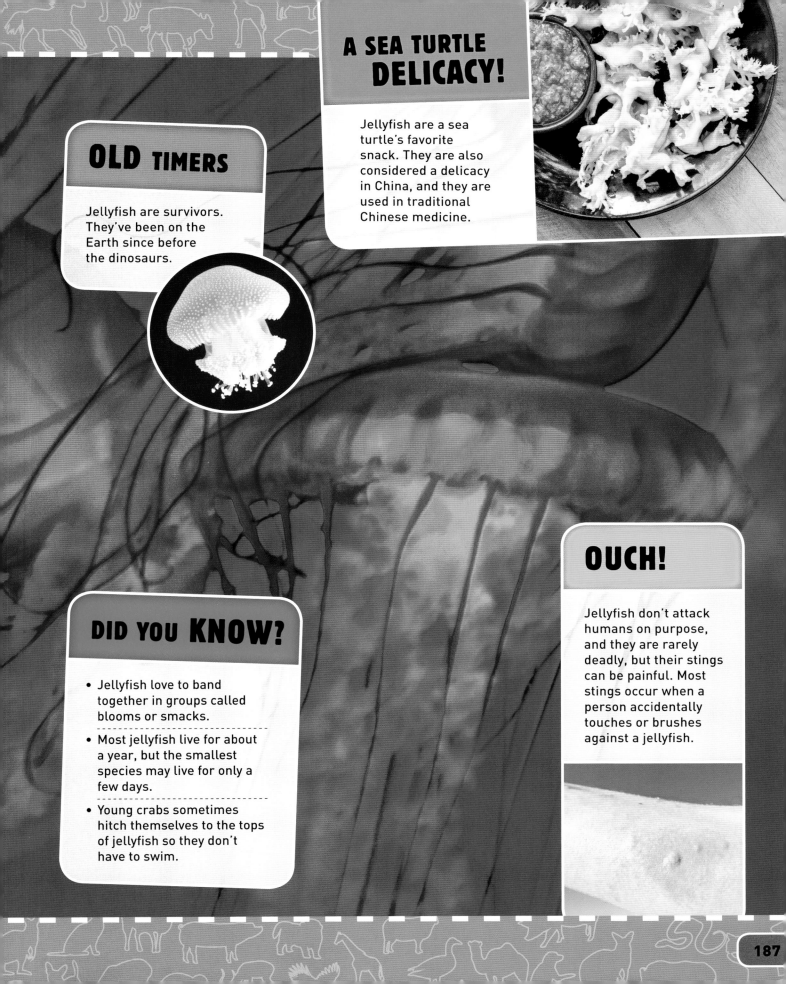

OLD TIMERS

Jellyfish are survivors. They've been on the Earth since before the dinosaurs.

A SEA TURTLE DELICACY!

Jellyfish are a sea turtle's favorite snack. They are also considered a delicacy in China, and they are used in traditional Chinese medicine.

DID YOU KNOW?

- Jellyfish love to band together in groups called blooms or smacks.
- Most jellyfish live for about a year, but the smallest species may live for only a few days.
- Young crabs sometimes hitch themselves to the tops of jellyfish so they don't have to swim.

OUCH!

Jellyfish don't attack humans on purpose, and they are rarely deadly, but their stings can be painful. Most stings occur when a person accidentally touches or brushes against a jellyfish.

Awesomely Bizarre Fish

LET'S GET CRAZY!

With more than 24,000 species of fish in the sea, some of them can be downright weird. Here's a look at some of nature's strangest underwater creations.

Red lionfish are hungry creatures. If left alone, they will eat and eat until all the small fish along the barrier reef are gone. That's why more than 300 scuba divers in the Cayman Islands have been certified to catch as many red lionfish as possible around the islands' famous coral reefs.

The **tasseled scorpionfish** of the Indian and Pacific Oceans is not to be messed with—it is carnivorous and venomous.

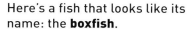

Here's a fish that looks like its name: the **boxfish**.

Frogfish can be found in tropical and subtropical oceans.

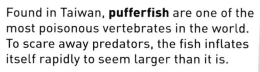

Found in Taiwan, **pufferfish** are one of the most poisonous vertebrates in the world. To scare away predators, the fish inflates itself rapidly to seem larger than it is.

Coral Reefs
IN LIVING **COLOR**

IT'S **ALIVE!**

When you lift coral out of the water, the hard shell you see is the animal's exoskeleton. The shell of a single coral is called a corallite. Inside the corallite sits the soft body of the coral, called a polyp. A coral reef is formed when groups of polyps grow together, creating different shapes and patterns.

Coral reefs are teeming with life. In fact, coral is a living organism, a relative of jellyfish and anemone. Since a coral reef needs sunlight to grow, it hardly ever grows in water deeper than 230 feet (70 meters). Coral also thrives in tropical oceans, where the water is warmer. Coral reefs make up some of the world's most interesting and diverse ecosystems, providing a home for thousands of species of fish and underwater plant life.

DID YOU KNOW?

- Compounds harvested from coral can be used to make medicines, including new treatments for cancer.
- Fish swim and lay eggs in coral reefs, where the eggs are protected. This fact makes reefs very important to the fishing industry.
- Seagrass is a sea plant that thrives under the protection of the coral reef. The seabed is more stable when more plants are growing on it. They stop the bottom of the bed from being washed out.
- Reefs grow better where there are stronger wave patterns and currents to wash in food.
- Fringing reefs are found closer to shore. Barrier reefs exist farther out to sea, in deeper waters.
- Coral reefs take up less than 1% of the ocean floor but support 25% of life in the ocean.

THE GREAT BARRIER REEF

The largest coral reef in the world is in Australia. The Great Barrier Reef covers 1,600 miles (2,575 kilometers) and is made up of 2,900 smaller reefs. It crosses 900 islands.

Salmon

UPSTREAM SWIMMERS

Salmon are born in freshwater rivers and streams and then migrate to the saltwater ocean. Salmon are among the hardest-working animals on the planet. When they are ready to reproduce, these fish exhibit amazing strength—they swim from the ocean all the way back upstream to the spot where they were born! Once there, the female makes a depression in the riverbed and lays her eggs, which the male then fertilizes. After filling up to seven depressions with eggs, the salmon are so exhausted that many of them die. The few who live can repeat the process and spawn two or three more times.

LIFE IN THE SEA

Salmon can be found in the Atlantic Ocean, Pacific Ocean, and North America's Great Lakes. An adult salmon spends between one and four years living in the ocean. It's a tough life: Salmon are prime meals for seals, sea lions, walruses, and bears.

DID YOU **KNOW?**

- There are six species of Pacific salmon and one of Atlantic.
- When emerging from their eggs, all baby fish are called fry.
- Salmon carry an average of 2,500 eggs.
- Salmon travel up to 3,500 miles (5,633 km) to spawn.

COLOR MATCH

The appearance of salmon varies between species. Chum salmon are silvery blue with black spots on their sides. Cherry salmon have bright red stripes. Most salmon are one color in freshwater and a different color in saltwater.

Chum Salmon

HEART-
HEALTHY

Wild salmon are considered one of the healthiest fish to eat. They are rich in vitamins, minerals, and omega-3 fatty acids, which lower the risk of heart disease and certain cancers.

CHILLING IN WARM WATER

Residing in tropical waters, the manta ray has a large, flattened body whose center is called a disk. A reef manta ray measures about 11 feet (3 meters) across. A giant oceanic manta ray can stretch to 23 feet (7 meters). Both species have eyes on the sides of their heads. Though manta rays are cousins of sharks, they are not carnivores; rather, their diet consists of tiny organisms called plankton. Despite having teeth, manta rays don't chew their food. Their gills have "gill rakers" that filter in the plankton and keep out the water. They really put their gill rakers to work, too: Every week, mantas consume around 12 percent of their body weight in food.

Manta Rays

Manta rays are ovoviviparous animals. You might need to repeat that word—slowly. Ovoviviparous refers to how some fish and reptile species give birth. Eggs are hatched within the body, so the young are born alive but without an attachment to the mother.

DID YOU KNOW?

- Manta rays are pretty smart; they have the largest brain of any fish in the sea.
- Manta rays have tiny teeth that are not good for chewing.
- Manta rays like warm water. They never migrate to chilly parts of the ocean.

BONELESS

The manta ray's skeleton is made of cartilage, not bone. You can feel cartilage right now—just touch the tip of your nose.

LUCKY TO BE LARGE

Manta rays aren't natural fighters. Luckily, they don't have many natural predators. And because they are large, most other fish stay away.

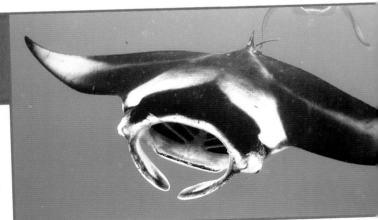

Pets

ANIMALS
COME HOME

People own pets all over the world. The U.S. leads the world in dog and cat ownership, with an estimated 90 million dogs and 94 million cats, according to the American Pet Products Association. Birds are most popular in Turkey, where 20 percent of people have a pet bird. Pet ownership rates are highest in Central America, though. According to one survey, nearly 80 percent of people in Argentina and Mexico own pets. That's a lot of balls to throw, terrariums to clean, and pet food to buy!

Pet History
Scientists have used the fossil record to find clues about the history of pets. Here are some of their most interesting findings.

10,000 BCE

In what is now Israel, a puppy is buried with its owner.

7500 BCE

An African wildcat is buried with a human on the island of Cyprus.

3000 BCE

The ancient Egyptians paint pictures of their house cats.

Adult cats don't meow to communicate with other cats—they do it to talk to people. Cats are very good at changing their meows to let their human owners know what they want to say. An early-morning "Feed me!" meow sounds very different from a friendly, "I'm happy you're home from school!" meow.

MAN'S BEST FRIEND

Greger Larson is a scientist leading a team that is trying to determine the origin of dog-human relationships. "We know that dogs, without a doubt, were the first domestic animal," Larson says. He means that dogs were the first animals that were tamed and used for work. But were dogs the first pets? That remains unclear. After years of research, scientists still aren't sure who man's first best friend was. A dog? A cat? Some other animal? "Nobody really knows," Larson says.

168-190 CE

Chinese Emperor Ling gives his dogs the rank of senior court officials.

1493 CE

Christopher Columbus brings Queen Isabella a pair of Cuban parrots as a gift.

1860 CE

The first commercially produced dog food is introduced in Britain.

1916 CE

The world's first Seeing Eye dogs are trained in Germany.

SUPER SKILLS

Cats have quick reflexes, sharp, extendable claws, and teeth perfect for killing mice and birds. Cats hear sounds that are too high for human ears, see in almost complete darkness, and possess a great sense of smell. They also love to scratch rough surfaces, jump into boxes, and bat around anything they can find.

Cats
MEOW ARE YOU?

Cats have cuddled up with humans for thousands of years. Ancient Egyptians worshipped cats, and some mummified them so their feline friends would have a smooth trip to the afterworld. Believe it or not, some owners mummified mice, too—just in case their cat got hungry in the next life!

- The heaviest known house cat weighed in at nearly 50 lbs. (22.7 kg).
- Cats can pass their bodies through any space through which they can fit their heads.
- Cats live about 12 to 15 years.
- There are between 200 and 600 million cats in the world today.

Siamese Cat

Persian Cat

A Breed Apart

There are many cat breeds.
Here is a look at some of them.

Bengal Cat

American Shorthair

Ragamuffin Cat

Bombay Cat

Dogs

BEST FRIENDS
FOREVER

Dogs have been running and playing alongside humans for 30,000 years. Today, every breed of dog, from a giant German shepherd to a dainty miniature poodle, is an integral part of someone's life. Scientists believe they have figured out why: Dogs and humans both share areas of their brains that are dedicated to voice recognition. The two species have been able to communicate vocally to each other, and those "talks" led to friendship. By nature, dogs are friendly and loyal. They are social creatures that like to be petted and walked, and love to run in the yard, the park, or just about anywhere. No wonder they are considered man's best friend!

DID YOU KNOW?

Some scientists believe that all dog breeds began with one species of gray wolf.

Beagle

Labrador Retriever

Dachshund

KNOW YOUR BREED!

Golden Retriever

Doberman Pinscher

Boxer

IT'S A HOWL

Dogs communicate in many ways. They bark and yap and wag their tails when they are happy. They whimper and tuck in their tails when scared. They growl when they are angry or defending their turf.

FAMILY TREE

Domestic dogs share traits with their wild ancestors. Dogs and wolves both mark their territories by urinating on trees, rocks, and fence posts—this lets other animals know that the dog or wolf has claimed a particular piece of land. Many dogs bury bones or other toys. Some bury meat for later meals.

Pets come in all shapes and sizes, and many people prefer the ones that are small, quiet, and fit in your hand. Say hello to the world of gerbils, hamsters, guinea pigs, and rabbits.

Smaller Pets

CUTE AND CUDDLY

A **guinea pig**, also known as a cavy, is a rodent that is native to the Andes Mountains. These small creatures are related to hamsters and gerbils. They were first domesticated around 3500 BCE by the Incas. In the 1500s, guinea pigs were brought to Europe as pets and laboratory animals. Today, the guinea pig makes a fine pet and can be found in kindergarten classrooms across the U.S. If a guinea pig is treated well, it will be a friendly companion for a long time. Some guinea pigs have been known to live for nine years.

Hamsters Make Fun Pets!

- Hamsters are rodents.
- There are 25 species of hamsters.
- Hamsters live in burrows. They are crepuscular, which means they come out at twilight to feed.
- Hamsters use their large cheeks to carry food back to their burrows.
- Hamsters can be black, gray, honey, white, brown, yellow, or red.

In the wild, **gerbils** live in an extensive network of tunnels and burrows, leading to food stores, nesting sites, and escape routes. At home in a cage or a tank, a gerbil will still need to burrow. They love to thump their strong back legs, hoard food, and gnaw pieces of wood. Gerbils also love company. You can try to adopt two gerbils from the same family, or you could get your gerbil a pal—you'll just have to keep them in separate places until they get used to each other. Gerbils are tidy and will keep their cage or tank clean longer than most other rodents.

Team Rabbit!

- Rabbits are very quiet.
- Rabbits have distinct personalities.
- Rabbits bond easily with their owners. Not all rabbits like to be picked up or held, though.
- Rabbits can be kept in relatively small cages but should be allowed to roam the house for at least a few hours a day.
- Rabbits can live up to 12 years in a home.
- Rabbits are clean.
- Rabbits are supercute!

Look-alikes

SOME SAY THAT DOGS LOOK LIKE THEIR OWNERS.

SOME SAY THAT **ALL** PETS LOOK LIKE THEIR OWNERS.

WHAT DO YOU THINK?

Parrots, CAN WE TALK?
Parakeets,
and Canaries

A talking pet is a pretty incredible thing. But along with their unique ability to speak, parrots and parakeets have other features that make them amazing pets.

DID YOU **KNOW?**

- There are almost 400 species of parrots.
- Parrots are some of the most intelligent birds on the planet.
- Some parrots can outlive their owners! These birds have been known to live up to 80 years.
- Parrots live mostly on seeds, but some eat fruit, flowers, and small insects.

New Zealand is home to some of the world's most unique parrots. These include the kea, kaka, and kakapo. Keas are the world's only alpine parrot and are known to create mischief around ski slopes. Kakapos are flightless parrots; sometimes, they are called the owl parrot for their owl-like bodies and large eyes. While there were once thousands of kakapos in New Zealand, they are now endangered.

Sing Like a Canary

- Song canaries love to vocalize and sometimes compete in singing competitions!

- Colorbred canaries come in up to 45 different colors. There are even colorbred competitions, in which the birds are judged on their plumage and beauty.

DID YOU **KNOW?**

- Never keep a canary in a room warmer than 85°F (29.4°C).

- Keep a new canary away from other birds for at least 3 weeks.

- Choose a cage big enough to allow your canary proper exercise.

- If a male lives in its own cage, he will more easily develop his song.

- With proper care, a canary can live for up to 15 years.

DID YOU **KNOW?**

- The word "parakeet" means "long tail."

- Parakeets come from Australia. Their natural plumage is yellow and green.

- Parakeets can speak. Some know up to 1,000 words!

- A parakeet's beak grows up to 3 in (7.6 cm) a year.

The Goshawk

BIRDS OF PREY

Raptors, or birds of prey, might seem like an unusual choice for a pet, but they've been living with humans for thousands of years. One of the most common is the goshawk, a medium-large raptor. The name "goshawk" evolved from the words "goose hawk" and refers to the bird's plumage as well as its skill as a fierce hunter.

FALCONRY

People have used birds of prey for hunting and sport for centuries. The bond of a master to his or her falcon is deep. The rules of the sport have changed very little over the years. Here's how it works:

- Falconers raise birds and train them to catch a variety of prey.
- Falconers who use goshawks train their birds to hunt other birds, as well as rabbits and small mammals.
- Falconers wear heavy leather gloves, which the bird uses for takeoff and landing.
- Falconers use food, usually meat, to train their birds to return to their glove.
- Birds often wear hoods to keep them calm before the hunt.

THAT'S DEDICATION!

There is no such thing as a casual falconer. Goshawks and other birds of prey are large, aggressive, and difficult to care for. Many falconers spend hours each day taking care of their birds and training them to hunt.

Fish as Pets

LIFE IN A BOWL

A fish can be a great starter pet, especially if you don't have time to walk a dog or change a cat's litter. Here are some of the easiest fish to care for.

COLD-WATER FISH

Goldfish

White Cloud Mountain Minnow

- Won at many county fairs, **goldfish** come in a variety of shapes and sizes, some with fancy tails.
- **Bloodfin tetras** are easy to care for and can live in some tanks up to 10 years.
- A **white cloud mountain minnow** likes cold water, indoors or out. Some people keep these minnows in outdoor ponds.

WARM-WATER FISH

- **Danios** are a great first fish because they do well in a variety of conditions and aren't picky eaters.
- The **black molly** is a peaceful fish. It's a good choice if you want a tank with several different species.
- **Black skirt tetras** are best owned in pairs. They like company.
- **Platies** are a great beginner fish because there are many varieties to choose from.
- **Swordtails** have a long bottom fin that looks like a sword.
- **Betta fish** add a dash of color to any tank. The males have beautifully colorful fins. But watch out—male betta fish like to fight, so you can have only one in a tank.

Black Molly

Swordtail

Betta Fish

Saltwater Fish
SIMPLY GORGEOUS!

Firefish are considered great for beginners because they will eat almost any food. Since they are small, a firefish can be kept in a 10-gallon (38-liter) tank. Be careful, though—firefish like to jump. Keep a hood on your aquarium to make sure they don't leap out!

Can a beginner keep a saltwater fish tank? Yes, but it takes work! First of all, saltwater fish usually need big aquariums that hold a minimum of 30 gallons (114 liters). Even with all that space to swim and hide out, some tropical fish don't get along. It's important to make sure that the species you pick are compatible. The tank's water temperature has to be strictly monitored, too. Even so, keeping a tropical fish tank can be incredibly rewarding. You can fill your reef aquarium with rocks and coral to make a complete underwater ecosystem. Your fish will love it!

The **blue-green chromis fish** likes company and does best with four or five pals in the tank. Known to be friendly, this finny friend tends to make nervous fish relax.

Besides looking extremely cool, **clownfish** swim by bobbing up and down in the water. Easy to keep, they eat most kinds of marine food.

Blennies and **gobies** are small fish that play well with others. They're easy to feed and help control algae.

Crabs are invertebrates that can fit in well with a beginner's saltwater tank. There are different species to choose from, too: hermit crabs, arrow crabs, or porcelain crabs.

Damselfish are usually the first fish to get for your new tropical tank. Along with being the least expensive fish on the market, they are very sturdy. But be careful: The damsel grows more aggressive as it gets larger.

The **captive-bred Kaudern's cardinal fish** has a silver body with black stripes and small white spots. This fish might hide when first placed in your aquarium. But don't worry—it will come out to eat.

DID YOU KNOW?

- Not all saltwater fish are the same. Aside from coming in a range of colors and sizes, some eat meat, some eat plants, and some eat both.

- Unlike freshwater fish, saltwater fish drink water.

- Saltwater fish are capable of using all five senses: sight, hearing, smell, touch, and taste.

Exotic Pets

BRING ON THE WEIRD!

Most people are content to have a dog or a cat as an animal companion, but some people go for the truly exotic. If you're thinking about getting an exotic pet, though, you'll need to use caution. Most exotic pets have a special diet and special needs. Also, check out your state's laws and regulations about exotic-pet ownership.

The **hissing cockroach**? Some people keep a bug as a pet? Yup!

Yes, **hedgehogs** are covered with spikes and like to stay up all night. But they sure are adorable!

Pigs for house pets? Some people love them. They are cleaner than their reputations would lead you to believe. Make sure you have room for them, though: Even miniature pigs get pretty big.

It may look fierce, but the **bearded dragon** (also called the *Pogona*) is calm and friendly.

The **Burmese python** can grow up to 17 feet (5 meters). They eat small mammals whole. If you decide to have a pet python, it's best *not* to have any other pets.

Some people think **tarantulas** look terrifying, but owners love them as pets. Despite their scary looks, tarantulas are pretty harmless.

Pet Etiquette

MINDING YOUR CATS AND DOGS

No one likes a neighbor who lets his dog bark all night. It's important to be a considerate pet owner, and that means knowing pet-owner etiquette. Treat your pets and your neighbors with respect, and everybody wins.

KNOCK, KNOCK!

Your doorbell rings, and guests arrive at your house. Are they afraid of dogs? It might be time to put your dog in another room for a while or let your dog outside to run in the yard. Don't worry, its feelings won't be hurt.

DOG OWNER 101

- Scoop the poop. Bring several bags on your dog walks so you can easily dispose of your dog's waste.

- Leash your dog when you go for a walk. In most cities, it's the law.

- Train your dog so they don't bark at people or other dogs.

- Dogs are social animals and need company, so make sure you don't leave your dog alone for long periods of time.

HORSE SENSE

Horse riding requires etiquette. The most important thing is to be good to your horse. It will need rest breaks and water, especially on hot days. Here are a few more tips:

- If your route is going to take you over private land, get permission from the owner first.

- Leave all gates as you found them. If you open a gate on your ride, close it after you.

- When taking a rest, try not to let your horse trample delicate plants. Be sure to scatter any manure piles before you leave.

- Pick up your litter.

- Don't tailgate. Even if your horse is fast, try to keep off the rear end of the horse in front.

Index

INDEX

CREDITS

For each page, photo credits are listed from left to right.

Front Cover: Ron_Thomas/istock/
Getty Images
Back Cover: adogslifephoto/istock/
Getty Images
Back Cover: Evgnil1/istock/Getty Images
Back Cover: zatrokz/istock/Getty Images
2: adogslifephoto/istock/Getty Images
2: AlexRaths/istock/Getty Images
3: MirasWonderland/istock/Getty Images
3: sidneybernstein/istock/Getty Images
3: sturti/istock/Getty Images
4: guenterguni/istock/Getty Images
4: GlobalP/istock/Getty Images
4: Inhauscreative/istock/Getty Images
5: GlobalP/istock/Getty Images
5: Stuartb/istock/Getty Images
5: GlobalP/istock/Getty Images
6: Fleckus/istock/Getty Images
7: eROMAZe/istock/Getty Images
7: ksumano/istock/Getty Images
8: SKapl/istock/Getty Images
9: Gannet77/istock/Getty Images
9: Zoran Kolundzija/istock/Getty Images
9: sculder19/istock/Getty Images
10: Kandfoto/istock/Getty Images
11: valdecasas/istock/Getty Images
11: MarkBeckwith/istock/Getty Images
12: User10095428_393/istock/Getty Images
13: Dimos_istock/istock/Getty Images
13: LindaMore/istock/Getty Images
13: ChrisHepburn/istock/Getty Images
15: guenterguni/istock/Getty Images
15: Freder/istock/Getty Images
15: LaserLens/istock/Getty Images
15: RobertH82/istock/Getty Images
16: ddea/istock/Getty Images
16: LuismiCSS/istock/Getty Images
16: BLMMACSBHGRF02/istock/Getty Images
16: RobHainer/istock/Getty Images
17: EvanTravels/istock/Getty Images
18: webguzs/istock/Getty Images
19: Tony Hisgett/CC BY 2.0
19: Gleb_Ivanov/istock/Getty Images
19: kjorgen/istock/Getty Images
19: vencavolrab/istock/Getty Images
19: Jorisvo/istock/Getty Images
20: 1001slide/istock/Getty Images
20: fotoslaz/istock/Getty Images
21: Africadventures/istock/Getty Images
21: Zoran Kolundzija/istock/Getty Images
23: mrakos/istock/Getty Images
22: pum_eva/istock/Getty Images
22: Leopardinatree/istock/Getty Images
23: Africanway/istock/Getty Images
24: MattiaATH/istock/Getty Images
24: skilpad/istock/Getty Images
25: yongkiet/istock/Getty Images
27: Etienne_Outram/istock/Getty Images
27: Gerrit_de_Vries/istock/Getty Images
27: Kyslynskyy/istock/Getty Images
27: EcoPic/istock/Getty Images
27: Binty/istock/Getty Images
28: WLDavies/istock/Getty Images
28: Photoservice/istock/Getty Images
28: Byrdyak/istock/Getty Images
29: zhengvision/istock/Getty Images
30: Dominique-Grosse/istock/Getty Images
31: eyalcohen/istock/Getty Images
31: BackyardProduction/istock/Getty Images
32: EMPPhotography/istock/Getty Images
33: chuvipro/istock/Getty Images
33: 5cheherazade/istock/Getty Images
33: Oktay Ortakcioglu/istock/Getty Images
34: EcoPic/istock/Getty Images
34: narvikk/istock/Getty Images
35: znm/istock/Getty Images
35: Kenneth Canning/istock/Getty Images
35: Ivan_Sabo/istock/Getty Images
35: WLDavies/istock/Getty Images
35: JurgaR/istock/Getty Images
36: belizar73/istock/Getty Images
37: Anolis01/istock/Getty Images
37: GlobalP/istock/Getty Images
37: Farinosa/istock/Getty Images
37: GNNick/istock/Getty Images
38: Aunt_Spray/istock/Getty Images
39: aleks1949/istock/Getty Images
39: Aunt_Spray/istock/Getty Images
39: CoreyFord/istock/Getty Images
40: pierivb/istock/Getty Images
40: nikpal/istock/Getty Images
40: Sami Sert/istock/Getty Images
41: dennisvdw/istock/Getty Images
41: Tony_Herbert/istock/Getty Images
41: reptiles4all/istock/Getty Images
41: Andrea Izzotti/istock/Getty Images
41: GlobalP/istock/Getty Images
42: Thanmano/istock/Getty Images
42: NTCo/istock/Getty Images
42: NNehring/istock/Getty Images
42: nok6716/istock/Getty Images
42: pchoui/istock/Getty Images
43: borchee/istock/Getty Images
43: Paul_roberts/istock/Getty Images
43: EMPPhotography/istock/Getty Images
43: andy2673/istock/Getty Images
43: klausbalzano/istock/Getty Images
43: Enjoylife2/istock/Getty Images
44: DmitryND/istock/Getty Images
44: Dgwildlife/istock/Getty Images
44: HuntedDuck/istock/Getty Images
44: jamcgraw/istock/Getty Images
45: jhorrocks/istock/Getty Images
45: Rumo/istock/Getty Images
46: GlobalP/istock/Getty Images
46: akinshin/istock/Getty Images
47: SeppFriedhuber/istock/Getty Images
47: SylvieBouchard/istock/Getty Images
48: karlumbriaco/istock/Getty Images
48: iChip/istock/Getty Images
48: GreatJoe/istock/Getty Images
48: Andyworks/istock/Getty Images
48: thejack/istock/Getty Images
50: arjayphotography/istock/Getty Images
51: tap10/istock/Getty Images
51: markrhiggins/istock/Getty Images
51: voodoopics/istock/Getty Images
51: CraigRJD/istock/Getty Images
51: akrp/istock/Getty Images
51: BerndC/istock/Getty Images
51: JohnCarnemolla/istock/Getty Images
52: GlobalP/istock/Getty Images
52: Hiro1775/istock/Getty Images
53: LeeYiuTung/istock/Getty Images
53: guenterguni/istock/Getty Images
54: GlobalP/istock/Getty Images
55: GeorgePeters/istock/Getty Images
55: janossygergely/istock/Getty Images
55: GlobalP/istock/Getty Images
56: luvemakphoto/istock/Getty Images
57: Zocha_K/istock/Getty Images
57: Wellcome Library, London/CC BY 4.0
57: DamianKuzdak/istock/Getty Images
57: rpbirdman/istock/Getty Images
58: zatrokz/istock/Getty Images
59: tulissidesign/istock/Getty Images
59: sarkophoto/istock/Getty Images
60: miketanct/istock/Getty Images
61: davidrasmus/istock/Getty Images
61: BirdImages/istock/Getty Images
61: FRANKHILDEBRAND/istock/Getty Images
61: wrangel/istock/Getty Images
61: GoodOlga/istock/Getty Images
61: gnagel/istock/Getty Images
61: Denisapro/istock/Getty Images
61: Andyd/istock/Getty Images
61: ghrushev/istock/Getty Images
62: JohanWElzenga/istock/Getty Images
64: kostolom/istock/Getty Images
64: twphotos/istock/Getty Images
64: EEI_Tony/istock/Getty Images
64: ingevdmeeberg/istock/Getty Images
64: erniedecker/istock/Getty Images
65: flySnow/istock/Getty Images
65: imagegrafx/istock/Getty Images
65: JohnPitcher/istock/Getty Images
65: NickBiemans/istock/Getty Images
65: carbonero/istock/Getty Images
65: zaricm/istock/Getty Images
66: genekrebs/istock/Getty Images
66: AzmanL/istock/Getty Images
66: pelooyen/istock/Getty Images
66: georgeclerk/istock/Getty Images
67: NikiTaxidisPhotography/istock/
Getty Images
67: Zoran Kolundzija/istock/Getty Images
67: SolStock/istock/Getty Images
67: Callipso/istock/Getty Images
68: esvetleishaya/istock/Getty Images
69: FedevPhoto/istock/Getty Images
69: emholk/istock/Getty Images
69: merlinpf/istock/Getty Images
70: Buffy1982/istock/Getty Images
71: michelangeloop/istock/Getty Images
71: SerrNovik/istock/Getty Images
71: GlobalP/istock/Getty Images
72: Callipso/istock/Getty Images
73: marlenka/istock/Getty Images
73: Callipso/istock/Getty Images
74: fomengto/istock/Getty Images
74: esemelwe/istock/Getty Images
75: SolStock/istock/Getty Images
75: GlobalP/istock/Getty Images
75: georgeclerk/istock/Getty Images
76: aerostato/istock/Getty Images
76: aydinmutlu/istock/Getty Images
77: borchee/istock/Getty Images
78: Display/istock/Getty Images
78: traveler1116/istock/Getty Images
79: Grafissimo/istock/Getty Images
79: Freder/istock/Getty Images
80: taxzi/istock/Getty Images
80: anopdesignstock/istock/Getty Images
81: DaydreamsGirl/istock/Getty Images
81: Tsekhmister/istock/Getty Images
82: chrisboy2004/istock/Getty Images
83: Antonio Gravante/istock/Getty Images
83: UroshPetrovic/istock/Getty Images
83: GlobalP/istock/Getty Images
83: ArmanWerthPhotography/istock/
Getty Images
83: mauribo/istock/Getty Images
84: georgeclerk/istock/Getty Images
84: DebbiSmirnoff/istock/Getty Images
85: IsaacRuiz/istock/Getty Images
85: suriyasilsaksom/istock/Getty Images
86: inhauscreative/istock/Getty Images
87: BreatheFitness/istock/Getty Images
87: AaronAmat/istock/Getty Images
87: GlobalP/istock/Getty Images
87: Ocs_12/istock/Getty Images
88: Peopleimages/Getty Images
88: Frank Glaw, Jörn Köhler, Ted M.
Townsend, Miguel Vences/CC BY 2.5
89: Stella Nutella at English Wikipedia/
CC BY-SA 3.0, CC BY 2.5
89: Rittmeyer EN, Allison A, Gründler MC,
Thompson DK, Austin CC/CC BY 2.5.
89: Blair Hedges, Penn State [Attribution], via
Wikimedia Commons.
90: SensorSpot/istock/Getty Images
91: GlobalP/istock/Getty Images
91: Mark Kostich/istock/Getty Images
91: Byronsdad/istock/Getty Images
91: unclegene/istock/Getty Images
91: carlosalvarez/istock/Getty Images
91: ShaneMyersPhoto/istock/Getty Images
91: Viktoryia Voinakh/istock/Getty Images
92: GlobalP/istock/Getty Images
92: GlobalP/istock/Getty Images
93: pokosuke/istock/Getty Images
93: 80s_girl/istock/Getty Images
93: roc8jas/istock/Getty Images
93: Cay-Uwe/istock/Getty Images
93: rkhalil/istock/Getty Images
93: huronphoto/istock/Getty Images
93: BrianEKushner/istock/Getty Images
94: adogslifephoto/istock/Getty Images
94: AHDesignConcepts/istock/Getty Images
95: MoMorad/istock/Getty Images
95: fenkieandreas/istock/Getty Images
95: stevelenzphoto/istock/Getty Images
95: StuPorts/istock/Getty Images
96: amwu/istock/Getty Images
96: alexeys/istock/Getty Images
97: t_cherdchay/istock/Getty Images
97: showcake/istock/Getty Images
97: Hoatzinexp/istock/Getty Images
98: Snowleopard1/istock/Getty Images
98: Saddako/istock/Getty Images
98: GlobalP/istock/Getty Images
98: zhnger/istock/Getty Images
99: Saddako/istock/Getty Images
100: Farinosa/istock/Getty Images
101: Stopboxstudio/istock/Getty Images
101: vlad61/istock/Getty Images
101: RainervonBrandis/istock/Getty Images
101: EcoPic/istock/Getty Images
102: Donyanedomam/istock/Getty Images
102: yschiu/istock/Getty Images
103: GlobalP/istock/Getty Images
102: Shumba138/istock/Getty Images
103: SomeSense/istock/Getty Images
103: DavidByronKeener/istock/Getty Images
103: ClaraNila/istock/Getty Images
103: Isaac74/istock/Getty Images
103: Westhoff/istock/Getty Images
104: GlobalP/istock/Getty Images
105: PiccoloNamek/CC BY-SA 3.0
105: MariSwanepoel/istock/Getty Images
105: reptiles4all/istock/Getty Images
106: Mustang_79/istock/Getty Images
107: 49pauly/istock/Getty Images
107: wojciech_gajda/istock/Getty Images
107: reptiles4all/istock/Getty Images
106: Mustang_79/istock/Getty Images
107: 49pauly/istock/Getty Images
107: wojciech_gajda/istock/Getty Images
107: reptiles4all/istock/Getty Images
108: Anest/istock/Getty Images
108: DieterMeyrl/istock/Getty Images
109: popphoto2526/istock/Getty Images
109: redhumv/istock/Getty Images
109: Henrik_L/istock/Getty Images
110: OGphoto/istock/Getty Images
110: stanley45/istock/Getty Images
110: Havana1234/istock/Getty Images
111: Okea/istock/Getty Images
111: elthar2007/istock/Getty Images
112: Scott Biales/istock/Getty Images
113: allgord/istock/Getty Images
114: Avalon_Studio/istock/Getty Images
114: Anest/istock/Getty Images
114: Joesboy/istock/Getty Images
115: epantha/istock/Getty Images
115: Hailshadow/istock/Getty Images
115: sasel77/istock/Getty Images
116: next143/istock/Getty Images
116: next143/istock/Getty Images
117: next143/istock/Getty Images
117: fcafotodigital/istock/Getty Images
118: stephanie phillips/istock/Getty Images
118: Atelopus/istock/Getty Images
119: Cabezonication/istock/Getty Images
119: Motionshooter/istock/Getty Images
119: coopder1/istock/Getty Images
119: KozyrevAnton/istock/Getty Images
120: jlmcloughlin/istock/Getty Images
121: Ockra/istock/Getty Images
121: bazilfoto/istock/Getty Images
121: Antagain/istock/Getty Images
121: Thomas Shanahan/istock/Getty Images
122: Nataba/istock/Getty Images
122: GlobalP/istock/Getty Images
122: AntiMartina/istock/Getty Images
123: nimblewit/istock/Getty Images
123: Neil_Burton/istock/Getty Images
123: jeanro/istock/Getty Images
123: SteveByland/istock/Getty Images
124: RichardSeeley/istock/Getty Images
125: AndreAnita/istock/Getty Images
125: Stuartb/istock/Getty Images
125: jerbarber/istock/Getty Images
127: summersetretrievers/istock/
Getty Images
127: atosf/istock/Getty Images
127: WilliamSherman/istock/Getty Images
127: NNehring/istock/Getty Images
127: iculizard/istock/Getty Images
127: rainyiris/istock/Getty Images
127: genesisgraphics/Getty Images
129: FRANKHILDEBRAND/istock/
Getty Images
128: DawnKey/istock/Getty Images
129: mycteria/istock/Getty Images
130: GlobalP/istock/Getty Images
131: ANNECORDON/istock/Getty Images
131: rusm/istock/Getty Images
132: nbiebach/istock/Getty Images
133: Jens_Lambert_Photography/istock/
Getty Images
133: sidneybernstein/istock/Getty Images
133: SteveOehlenschlager/istock/
Getty Images
134: pablo_rodriguez_merkel/istock/
Getty Images
134: gallinago_media/istock/Getty Images
135: Altinosmanaj/istock/Getty Images
135: zorazhuang/istock/Getty Images
136: szefei/istock/Getty Images
137: Serhan Oksay/CC BY-SA 3.0
137: Greg Schechter/CC BY 2.0
137: Kagenmi/istock/Getty Images
137: J. Wolf and J. Smith/Martijn Zegel
Teylers Museum/Public Domain
138: Zoran_Photo/istock/Getty Images
138: Zwilling330/istock/Getty Images
139: BrianAJackson/istock/Getty Images
139: Missing35mm/istock/Getty Images
140: MindStorm-inc/istock/Getty Images
140: Kativ/istock/Getty Images
141: EarnestTse/istock/Getty Images
141: pchoui/istock/Getty Images
141: drferry/istock/Getty Images
142: DelmasLehman/istock/Getty Images
143: mcbrugg/istock/Getty Images
143: Spondylolithesis/istock/Getty Images
143: mbolina/istock/Getty Images
144: Bobbushphoto/istock/Getty Images
145: bazilfoto/istock/Getty Images
144: benedek/istock/Getty Images
145: johan63/istock/Getty Images
145: pchoui/istock/Getty Images
145: tracielouise/istock/Getty Images
145: Gary Gray/istock/Getty Images
145: Sjo/istock/Getty Images
145: Fireglo2/istock/Getty Images
146: Pekic/istock/Getty Images
147: jassmatass/istock/Getty Images
147: Markanja/istock/Getty Images
147: Antagain/istock/Getty Images
148: BirdImages/istock/Getty Images
148: MikeLane45/istock/Getty Images
149: Alphotographic/istock/Getty Images
149: 80s_girl/istock/Getty Images
149: PaulReevesPhotography/istock/
Getty Images
149: PaulReevesPhotography/istock/
Getty Images
149: Thom_Morris/istock/Getty Images
149: HelenWalkerz65/istock/Getty Images
150: CraigRJD/istock/Getty Images
151: MoMorad/istock/Getty Images
151: CraigRJD/istock/Getty Images
151: MoMorad/istock/Getty Images
151: Daderot/Public Domain
152: Antagain/istock/Getty Images
153: Jag_cz/istock/istock/Getty Images
153: TommL/istock/Getty Images
153: pixelnest/istock/Getty Images
153: Antagain/istock/Getty Images
154: tzooka/istock/Getty Images
154: Mathisa_s/istock/Getty Images
154: AttaBoyLuther/istock/Getty Images
154: leekris/istock/Getty Images
155: Liliboas/istock/Getty Images
156: emptyclouds/istock/Getty Images
156: BackyardProduction/istock/
Getty Images
157: tropper2000/istock/Getty Images
157: BarbaraStorms/istock/Getty Images
157: tropper2000/istock/Getty Images
158: GlobalP/istock/Getty Images
158: spxChrome/istock/Getty Images
159: Jab43120/istock/Getty Images
159: dreamnikon/istock/Getty Images
159: Akchamczuk/istock/Getty Images
159: phittavas/istock/Getty Images
159: stevegeer/istock/Getty Images
160: ApisitWilaijit/istock/Getty Images
160: Atelopus/istock/Getty Images
161: Attardog/istock/Getty Images
161: contrail1/istock/Getty Images
161: PeteMuller/istock/Getty Images
161: doug4537/istock/Getty Images
162: JGalione/istock/Getty Images
163: OGphoto/istock/Getty Images
163: RollingEarth/istock/Getty Images
163: yai112/istock/Getty Images
163: MBadnjar/istock/Getty Images
163: arlindo71/istock/Getty Images
163: tiwaongin/istock/Getty Images
164: Antagain/istock/Getty Images
165: Antagain/istock/Getty Images
165: Terryfic3D/istock/Getty Images
165: NNehring/istock/Getty Images
165: Antagain/istock/Getty Images
165: GlobalP/istock/Getty Images
166: Andrea Izzotti/istock/Getty Images
167: sollsuchstock/istock/Getty Images
167: hanhanpeggy/istock/Getty Images
167: astra490/istock/Getty Images
168: eco2drew/istock/Getty Images
168: blake81/istock/Getty Images
169: sethakan/istock/Getty Images
170: GlobalP/istock/Getty Images
170: eoind/istock/Getty Images
170: benedek/istock/Getty Images
171: Vasilvich/istock/Getty Images
171: pilipenkoD/istock/Getty Images
171: SoopySue/istock/Getty Images
173: mikeuk/istock/Getty Images
173: Leamus/istock/Getty Images
173: SeppFriedhuber/Getty Images
173: gaikphotos/istock/Getty Images
174: cynoclub/istock/Getty Images
175: tanuha2001/istock/Getty Images
175: reisegraf/istock/Getty Images
176: Krofoto/istock/Getty Images
176: s1murg/istock/Getty Images
177: EXTREME-PHOTOGRAPHER/istock/
Getty Images
178: USO/istock/Getty Images
179: RamonCarretero/istock/Getty Images
179: RamonCarretero/istock/Getty Images
179: lindsay_imagery/istock/Getty Images
180: Torchuck/istock/Getty Images
180: inusuke/istock/Getty Images
181: itsme23/istock/Getty Images
181: Subaqueosshutterbug/istock/
Getty Images
182: DPFishCo/istock/Getty Images
183: EJJohnsonPhotography/istock/
Getty Images
183: OscarMVargas/istock/Getty Images
184: Joesboy/istock/Getty Images
184: fusaromike/istock/Getty Images
184: RapidEye/istock/Getty Images
185: Mayehem/istock/Getty Images
186: ExhaustedResearch/istock/
Getty Images
187: tydiron/istock/Getty Images
187: armcreation/istock/Getty Images
187: borchee/istock/Getty Images
188: wrangel/istock/Getty Images
189: marrio31/istock/Getty Images
189: mikelillo/istock/Getty Images
189: semet/istock/Getty Images
189: FtLaudGirl/istock/Getty Images
189: borchee/istock/Getty Images
191: ltos/istock/Getty Images
191: Grafner/istock/Getty Images
192: Leamus/istock/Getty Images
192: PerfectStills/istock/Getty Images
193: AlexRaths/istock/Getty Images
193: Elena_Danileiko/istock/Getty Images
193: krisbasonphotography/istock/
Getty Images
194: MichaelStubblefield/istock/
Getty Images
195: crisod/istock/Getty Images
195: haveseen/istock/Getty Images
196: AndrilOliinyk/istock/Getty Images
196: Yobro10/istock/Getty Images
196: kali9/istock/Getty Images
196: NNehring/istock/Getty Images
196: VolNa69/istock/Getty Images
197: Pazhyna/istock/Getty Images
197: Alex Potemkin/istock/Getty Images
197: USO/istock/Getty Images
197: Sonsedska/istock/Getty Images
197: CSA-Printstock/istock/Getty Images
197: AnneMS/istock/Getty Images
197: apixel/Getty Images
198: Andypott/istock/Getty Images
198: flySnow/istock/Getty Images
199: igaguri_1/istock/Getty Images
199: chromatos/istock/Getty Images
199: KrissiLundgren/istock/Getty Images
199: rukawajung/istock/Getty Images
199: Zoran_Photo/istock/Getty Images
199: johan10/istock/Getty Images
199: 400tmax/istock/Getty Images
200: SensorSpot/istock/Getty Images
201: NORRIE3699/istock/Getty Images
201: fotokostic/istock/Getty Images
201: iamsom/istock/Getty Images
201: 1Tomm/istock/Getty Images
201: Anna-av/istock/Getty Images
201: MOAimages/istock/Getty Images
201: RinoCdZ/istock/Getty Images
202: DevMarya/istock/Getty Images
202: GlobalP/istock/Getty Images
202: DevMarya/istock/Getty Images
203: Hougaard/istock/Getty Images
203: artemisphoto/istock/Getty Images
203: Kerrick/istock/Getty Images
204: Rasulovs/istock/Getty Images
204: Roman_Baiadin/istock/Getty Images
204: Peopleimages/istock/Getty Images
204: PeskyMonkey/istock/Getty Images
205: Spiderstock/istock/Getty Images
205: knape/istock/Getty Images
205: brickrena/istock/Getty Images
206: istock-dk/istock/Getty Images
206: cusoncom/istock/Getty Images
207: OlhoFoto/istock/Getty Images
207: Thomas Demarczyk/istock/
Getty Images
208: Anolis01/istock/Getty Images
209: umdash9/istock/Getty Images
209: Andyworks/istock/Getty Images
210: mehmettorlak/istock/Getty Images
210: Mirko_Rosenau/istock/Getty Images
210: Jacob Wackerhausen/istock/
Getty Images
211: Jacob Wackerhausen/istock/
Getty Images
211: Mirko_Rosenau/istock/Getty Images
211: Jacob Wackerhausen/istock/
Getty Images
211: FYMStudio/istock/Getty Images
211: Dejan Kolar/istock/Getty Images
211: itthipolB/istock/Getty Images
211: sannse/CC BY-SA 3.0
211: Jacob Wackerhausen/istock/
Getty Images
211: Jacob Wackerhausen/istock/
Getty Images
212: vojce/istock/Getty Images
212: marrio31/istock/Getty Images
213: aon168/istock/Getty Images
213: wrangel/istock/Getty Images
213: Delpixart/istock/Getty Images
213: hocus-focus/istock/Getty Images
213: LagunaticPhoto/istock/Getty Images
214: pandpstock001/istock/Getty Images
214: kevdog818/istock/Getty Images
215: Byrdyak/istock/Getty Images
215: girishacf/istock/Getty Images
215: Lipowski/istock/Getty Images
215: Freder/istock/Getty Images
216: GlobalP/istock/Getty Images
216: adogslifephoto/istock/Getty Images
216: adogslifephoto/istock/Getty Images
217: adogslifephoto/istock/Getty Images
217: PeopleImages/istock/Getty Images
217: humonia/istock/Getty Images